A
Most Precious
Time

Finding Peace in the Midst of Tragedy

Mitch Pouliot

WESTBOW
PRESS®
A DIVISION OF THOMAS NELSON
& ZONDERVAN

Unless otherwise noted, scripture taken from the New King James Version®. Copyright © 1982 by Thomas Nelson. Used by permission. All rights reserved.

Scripture quotations marked (NIV) are taken from the Holy Bible, New International Version®, NIV®. Copyright © 1973, 1978, 1984, 2011 by Biblica, Inc.™ Used by permission of Zondervan. All rights reserved worldwide. www.zondervan.com The "NIV" and "New International Version" are trademarks registered in the United States Patent and Trademark Office by Biblica, Inc.™

Scripture quotations taken from the New American Standard Bible® (NASB), Copyright © 1960, 1962, 1963, 1968, 1971, 1972, 1973, 1975, 1977, 1995 by The Lockman Foundation Used by permission. www.Lockman.org

Scripture quotations marked (NLT) are taken from the Holy Bible, New Living Translation, copyright ©1996, 2004, 2015 by Tyndale House Foundation. Used by permission of Tyndale House Publishers, Inc., Carol Stream, Illinois 60188. All rights reserved.

WestBow Press books may be ordered through booksellers or by contacting:

WestBow Press
A Division of Thomas Nelson & Zondervan
1663 Liberty Drive
Bloomington, IN 47403
www.westbowpress.com
1 (866) 928-1240

ISBN: 978-1-9736-3999-2 (sc)
ISBN: 978-1-9736-4001-1 (hc)
ISBN: 978-1-9736-4000-4 (e)

Library of Congress Control Number: 2018911052

Print information available on the last page.

WestBow Press rev. date: 9/21/2018

To My Beloved Son Daniel John Pouliot

I cherish every moment that God blessed me with you.
And even though our days were short, a love-filled life shone through.
Your eyes, your smile, and gentle ways were such a joy to me.
Your kindness and compassion were always humbling.

I cherish every laugh and tear that made our hearts as one.
Not recognized as special then, our time had just begun.
Your shy and quiet ways would mask the wonder of your mind,
A genuine and caring heart to those patient to find.

I cherish every spoken word expressed to help you grow
In love and knowledge of our God, the one you longed to know.
Your faith was growing through it all, a treasure to behold,
A gift from God to help you trust and help you to let go.

I cherish every pain-filled day that you had to endure.
You taught me how to love this life and how to let it go.
My time with you, ordained by God, though I desired more,
So He showed me His special love for you, His cherished one.

Your days established and set forth are beautiful to God.
His book of life contains your name, a name I long to know.
And now you're with our Father God, a precious time to Him.
A son of God, you're welcomed into God's great family.

Cherished is this time to God, a view beyond my reach.
Please change my heart and make this be a precious time to me.

Contents

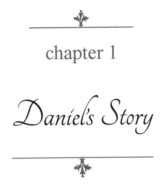

chapter 1

Daniel's Story

The summer of 2013 was a wonderful time for my wife, Gretchen, and me. Our older son, David, was prospering in his career and had just married the love of his life. Our younger son, Daniel, was in college but still uncommitted to his curriculum. As parents, the heavy lifting was behind us, so our focus was on helping Daniel find a career path that fit his interests and intellect.

Although his professional future was unclear, one thing was certain: Daniel loved to work out. He loved feeling the pump. It made him feel good about himself. I think he liked it when I talked about his pipes. One day as Daniel was working out with his good friend, the two of them noticed that his right arm was turning blue and swollen. They knew right away that something wasn't right, so that evening Gretchen took him to the emergency room.

After several hours, the doctors said they found clotting in Daniel's right shoulder. Since the vascular doctors wouldn't be in till morning, they sent Daniel home and told him he could come in the next morning for additional tests.

That September Friday was supposed to be a good day. The family had been planning on coming to our house for dinner to celebrate my birthday. The day, however, started out anything but good. After several more hours of tests and waiting in the emergency room, the doctors confirmed that Daniel had a blood clot in his upper arm, and they found several small blood clots on his lungs. We later learned that his condition was known as Paget-Schroetter syndrome. In layman's terms, it's a fairly rare condition in which blood clots form in the veins of the arm, caused by compression in the passageway from the lower neck to the armpit.

As we were processing the severity of Daniel's condition, he got a call on the emergency room phone. As he held the phone to his ear, I could see his expression change from casual listening to concern to distress. He passed the phone to me and said the doctor wanted to talk to me. The doctor explained that a blood test revealed that Daniel had all the markers for chronic lymphocytic leukemia (CLL). They would be sending the blood sample to the Mayo Clinic to verify their findings. It was routine for them to confirm this type of diagnosis, but it was especially necessary in Daniel's case because CLL was common in the elderly but uncommon in middle-aged adults and rarely—if ever—found in someone of Daniel's age.

My heart sank, but I knew I had to stay strong and positive for Daniel and Gretchen, who had their eyes glued to me as I hung up the phone. I recited what the doctor told me yet was struggling to process what I was saying. Needless to say, we were all in shock. It was surreal. Our first response was disbelief. How could this have happened? Was this a mistake? Did they mix Daniel's blood test with someone else's? Surely the blood test results from Mayo would clear up this gross mistake.

However, that never happened. The diagnosis was confirmed. Daniel had CLL.

Over the next few weeks, we were faced with several doctor visits, blood tests, and numerous other tests and evaluations to determine the next steps to address Daniel's clotting condition, as well as to understand the progression of the cancer and treatment options. The vascular surgeon removed the clot in Daniel's shoulder and put him on blood thinners. We were to wait until the clots in his lungs dissolved, and then he would be scheduled for surgery to remove the rib that was causing the restriction and trauma to his veins. We also met with two oncologists, one from the local hospital and one from a nearby hospital who had more expertise in the treatment of CLL. Both of them talked to us in clinical terms, telling us all the things that they knew about CLL and the treatments they could provide when the time came. With both of them, the conversation finally came to a point where they said there was nothing they could do to cure the disease. They said that, ultimately, Daniel would die from it.

Daniel eventually had the surgery to remove his rib and was then cleared to stop taking blood thinners. With that, the Paget-Schroetter syndrome was finally behind us. As for the CLL, the oncologist decided to meet with Daniel every three months because his white blood cell count wasn't increasing very rapidly. Daniel probably wouldn't need to start treatment, she said, for at least two years.

Over the next few years, things went back to normal (or settled into a new normal). Daniel was busy balancing school, part-time work, time with family and friends, and dating. The only times we thought about Daniel's condition were during his quarterly visits with the oncologist.

Come 2016, it was time to start treatment. Daniel's oncologist informed us of a novel clinical trial that was well suited for him. Key CLL markers indicated that this new trial would provide Daniel with an excellent prognosis. We were thrilled at the news! We waited as long as possible before having him start the trial—his life was so full that year with a wedding on the horizon!—and then in the fall, Daniel entered the trial.

As 2017 began, we were given the wonderful news we had been hoping and praying for. Daniel had no trace of the CLL in his bone marrow, his blood counts were back to normal levels, and his lymph nodes were no longer swollen. Daniel was done with the worst part of the trial. We were all looking forward to closing out the final months of treatment and putting this chapter of Daniel's life behind us.

But then came May, when things took an abrupt turn in the wrong direction. One evening, shortly after he had returned home from a routine hospital visit, Daniel started running a fever and was short of breath. Daniel's wife, Sarah, immediately took him to the emergency room. Once there, the doctors decided to keep him in the hospital overnight to evaluate his condition. Daniel's initial communication with Gretchen and me was that everything indicated that he was going to be okay.

Little did anyone realize at the time that Daniel's fever and shortness of breath were caused by congestive heart failure.

The diagnosis came quickly though. The cardiologist gave Daniel water pills and blood pressure medicine to make it easier for his heart to pump. After one more night of observation, he was sent home. The doctor said we would have to wait and see whether the medications worked. He told us that, at best, Daniel would be on these medications for the rest of his life, and at worst, he would need a heart transplant. At the time, we didn't recognize how serious the situation was. It was beyond our comprehension that another trial was at our doorstep. Given that Daniel was sent home with just pills, we were hoping for the best.

Over the next few weeks, Daniel made two trips to the emergency room. When he stood, he had extreme pain in his groin. When he sat or lay down, he had continuous pain in his abdomen. Then Daniel started vomiting, so Sarah took him to the emergency room for a third time. At that point, they finally did a CAT scan and told us that the pain was because his abdomen was full of fluid and he was getting fluid in his lungs. The pain when he stood was caused by all that fluid from his abdomen rushing down into the groin. That same fluid was causing the pain in his abdomen when he sat or tried to lie down.

We came to the realization that Daniel was not getting the appropriate care at the local hospital, so we had him transported to a hospital that had more expertise in dealing with heart conditions. Even then—with Daniel having congestive heart failure, his medicines not working, his abdomen filling with fluids, and his organs swelling—we still didn't fully realize how bad his condition was. By the time he arrived at the new hospital, the ER doctors told us Daniel was in grave condition.

Daniel was transferred late that night to the cardiac intensive care unit (CICU), and over the next few days, the doctors tried to find a balance of drugs to reduce his blood pressure and make it easier for his heart to pump blood. The goal was to make it easier for his heart to support his body and to give it a chance to rebound. They were hopeful that his heart would improve and that they could then switch him to over-the-counter drugs that would allow him to go home.

As the days went by, the doctors did see some improvement in his heart capacity, but there was not enough to get him switched over to the less powerful over-the-counter drugs. They let us know that a heart transplant was being considered. By this time, Daniel welcomed the thought of having a transplant because his quality of life was so poor. It's hard to imagine welcoming such an invasive procedure with so many adverse side effects, so that told us how difficult it was for Daniel.

We continued to see very small improvements in Daniel's heart function, so we held onto that, hoping that every little change was a sign from God that He was there and healing Daniel. That hope was shattered though when the cardiologists informed us that they would not be recommending Daniel for transplant due to his history with cancer and blood clotting. They also let us know that Daniel would not be able to have any mechanical device to assist his heart since both sides of his heart were damaged and there wasn't a device that would support his condition. In essence, what they were telling us was that there was nothing more they could do for him.

The doctors reached out to other medical centers around the country that specialized in heart transplants to see if any would accept the risks associated with Daniel's condition. Cedars-Sinai Medical Center in California was willing to look at Daniel's medical history, once more elevating our hopes. However, this news was quickly tempered when it became apparent to the cardiologist that Daniel's condition had worsened to the point that he couldn't make the trip to California without some kind of intervention. He offered up two options that were risky but given the urgency of the situation needed to be considered. The first was an internal heart pump that would assist the heart. This was the best option, but there was a concern that Daniel's arteries wouldn't be large enough to feed the pump up to the heart. The second riskier device was an external pump called ECMO.

We immediately were in favor of whatever it would take to get Daniel to Cedars-Sinai, so we moved forward with the procedure to insert the internal heart pump. Daniel's cardiologist truly cared for Daniel's well-being, so he counseled us on how to be an advocate for Daniel and pushed the surgeons to support our request. Daniel was taken into surgery, but, as we knew was possible, Daniel's arteries were too small. The surgeons decided to place a less effective balloon pump in his heart, even though they knew that this type of pump would not provide enough support for his heart.

We were next told that the doctors would monitor Daniel's condition for a few hours to see how his heart responded to the balloon pump. They weren't expecting it to work, and if it wasn't enough, they would move to the next option: ECMO. Several hours went by, and as expected, the balloon pump wasn't adequate.

Daniel then had the surgery to connect him to ECMO, which was successful, but the surgeons decided to temporarily leave the balloon pump in as well. They kept him heavily sedated overnight, so when morning came, there wasn't any significant change in his condition. He was on ECMO, and it was adequately supporting his heart. The doctors decided to remove the balloon pump after all because they felt it was restricting blood flow in his leg. About that time, we got confirmation that Cedars-Sinai, the insurance company, and the hospital had worked out all the arrangements to get Daniel transported to California. We all breathed a huge sigh of relief and gathered to thank God for opening that last door.

With the hustle to pull together all travel arrangements underway, I decided to check on Daniel one more time before things got hectic again. I entered his room while the technician was just finishing up with the balloon pump removal and the nurses were going through their paces of monitoring him. All seemed normal, but then I noticed one of the nurses check his eyes, look up with a concerned look, and check his eyes again. She calmly but swiftly left the room and came back with the attending doctor. The doctor likewise checked his eyes and then left to get the surgeon, followed by the neurologist. I could tell something was very wrong, so I prayed a quiet prayer and went out to get Gretchen.

Before we knew it, the neurologist was bringing us all into a meeting room to tell us what was going on. One of Daniel's eyes was dilated, and the other wasn't. He explained the best possible outcome and the worst. They wanted to do a CT scan to understand how significant of a problem we were facing. The hour it took to get the results seemed like an eternity as we quietly paced and said silent prayers for God's protection and healing.

Finally, the doctor called us all back into the same meeting room, only this time the vascular surgery staff and neurology staff packed into the room with us. The chief neurologist spoke for the group. He told us the CT scan confirmed the worst-case scenario. Daniel had a large blood clot in his aorta that had cut off blood flow to one side of his brain. Daniel had suffered a massive stroke.

We spent the next seven hours waiting for family to get to the hospital to say their last goodbyes and processing what had just happened to Daniel.

Finally, it was time for us to remove Daniel from ECMO. The family encircled him as the machines were disconnected. We prayed that God would comfort Daniel and carry him home. Daniel's body slowly shut down, and Daniel left this world.

〃〃〃〃

What just happened? It was just a short time ago that we were celebrating Daniel's healing from the CLL. Why did it happen? Why would God be so intimately involved in Daniel's healing and then not heal him from this?

The fog was so thick. My mind couldn't comprehend the reality of what had just taken place. I felt pain but also numbness and confusion. I felt that God had turned His back on us. There were so many questions. How would I ever be able to trust God again? How could I believe and hope for any of God's promises if He breaks His promises for healing? If God's Word can't be trusted for healing, it can't be trusted for anything. I thought God loved us. I thought God loved Daniel!

These were my thoughts and my cries in those paralyzing moments following my son's death. Friend, can you relate? Because you're holding this book in your hands, I suspect you too have experienced grief. You probably have questions similar to mine and find yourself asking over and over again why God put your particular trial before you. Trusting in God, as you know, means letting go of all control, yet you can't bear to think about what you'll do if the trial's outcome isn't what you desire.

You're continually thrust into a cycle of discouragement, searching for answers, prayer, peace for the moment, and then discouragement again. This trial threatens to shake your faith. Even simple comments made to provide guidance for you, like "There's only so much that we can do" and "Prayer will only take you so far," are now enough to send you down the path of trying to take control of the situation and ignoring God.

Doors of hope open and close continuously. You've been riding an emotional roller coaster as you try with all your might to hold on to every positive result and not allow the negative results to bring you down.

There are good days with bright eyes, smiles, light conversation, and even joking with the hospital staff. In some ways, the hospital staff become family to you because of the care they're providing to your loved one.

There are days that aren't so good, when there is pain and discomfort or you receive news that isn't good, yet you hold on to the threads of positive news intertwined in the data dump the doctors unload on you.

And then there are bad days—days when the reality of what's in front of you cannot be ignored or compartmentalized. Some of those days are really dark; they bury you in sorrow and pain. Those are the days when you feel most alone and lost. You may be surrounded by loved ones, yet they can't take away this dark reality causing such pain deep within you. Everyone around you can bring comfort and support to your body. They can hug you, kiss you, prop you up, rub your back—external stuff. But they can't even access where the pain is. It's buried so deep in your soul that no words or contact can ever get there.

It's at these times when, even if you didn't communicate with God regularly, you're there now. Your heart tells you to call out to God. You want to trust that God wills what's best for you and your loved ones. However, you have doubts. You doubt that God heals, or if He does, that He will actually intervene in your loved one's life.

But even if you have the strongest of faith, when you're hit with the reality that you need to say goodbye to your loved one, nothing prepares you for the loss. You start off being confused and angry—angry at God for allowing this to happen.

I needed answers from God. I needed to know why. Why did God put Daniel through so much pain and suffering? As a parent, I needed to know that Daniel was okay, that he was being cared for and loved. You may not have all of the same questions I had, but we all share the same fundamental question: how could a loving God bring so much pain and suffering into our lives?

How do we make sense of the death of someone so dear to us, with their entire life in front of them? How do we truly understand God's promises for us and His will for us? Does God promise healing or doesn't He? Does God ever abandon us? Why should we pray? Where are our loved ones? Are they being cared for and loved?

As I've gone through this journey, I have discovered that there are answers, for me and for you. The pain you feel does not need to remain.

There is a way to move forward with your life in a way that honors the life of your loved one. That is what your loved one would want for you, and it is what God wants also. You see, our paradigms shape how we view death. While we look at death as loss, God views it as the next precious step in our lives.

Our loss is still there. That will never change. That loss is very personal. A very, very important part of us has been taken away, so we will never be the same again. Yet God has given me the peace and understanding to know that my beloved Daniel is alive and well and in a better place than I could ever have imagined.

So this is not a story with a tragic ending, and neither is your story. Our stories are love stories. God is not absent in your time of most need. God is there. When our care for our loved one has reached its fullness, God steps in and carries that love forward. So come, join me as we discover what God has in store for our loved ones in this wonderful, precious time.

chapter 2

Does God Give Us Trials?

"Be careful what you ask for; you just might get it." It's a simple old saying that continues to hang on because of its relevance in so many areas of life.

It was first said to me when I was called into God's family. As a young, passionate follower of Jesus, I was drawn to His Word and wanted to do everything in my power to be closer to Him. I remember more mature Christians affectionately warning me, though, to be careful what I asked for. Of course, I didn't listen. God puts the desire in our hearts for more intimacy with Him, so we often pray for that. However, we're seldom prepared for the changes and growth required for that intimacy. God knows our hearts better than anyone. He knows our strengths and weaknesses. He knows where He wants to take us and what it will take to get us there. So the things He puts before us will force us to change or grow in directions we're reluctant or refusing to go.

In my case, I was determined to spend more and more time in Bible study and prayer. Having a background in engineering, I decided to create a graph with time spent in prayer and Bible study on the vertical axis and days on the horizontal axis. Each day, I would plot how much time I spent in both. I even gave myself a target line with a positive slope. In other words, the target got harder and harder to achieve with each passing day. You can see where this is going, right?

It didn't take long for God to squash me like a bug. It became harder and harder for me to find any time to spend with Him, let alone meet my targets. There were issues at work, family commitments, and home projects that took up all of my waking hours. I became so frustrated. Finally, God intervened. God, in a not so subtle or quiet voice, told me to stop what I was doing immediately, that what I was doing was not what He wanted. This was not the kind of relationship He wanted with me. Setting targets? Really?

Through this, God taught me a valuable lesson about the type of relationship He *did* want with me—one that was based on love, and closeness, and intimacy. A relationship based on a desire to serve and please Him for who He is and what He has done for me. God wanted me to talk to Him not to fill a requirement or target I set but because I wanted to share my day with Him and wanted His help with all my issues. He wanted the kind of relationship with me that a parent has with their young child. Yet this didn't come about without a significant period of frustration because I wasn't able to get where I wanted to go. I felt disconnected from God, spiritually lost and alone. There was no joy or peace that came from prayer. I was finding it difficult to work through issues I was having. Even the simplest of decisions I needed to make became laborious to work through. The everyday events of life became a chore, so much so that I started becoming depressed and disconnected from my family.

God was using the desire I had within me to please Him and be close to Him to lead me into making changes in my attitude and perspective so that true intimacy with Him would be possible. All of us who are drawn to God experience these times of difficulty. They come in different ways for each of us, unique to our personalities and circumstances, but they do come.

These times of difficulty we go through as we walk with God are meant for our good. They are known as trials.

The Purpose of Trials

God puts trials in our lives because we are His children. The writer of Hebrews tells us, "For whom the Lord loves He chastens, and scourges every son whom He receives. If you endure chastening, God deals with you as with sons; for what son is there whom a father does not chasten?" (Heb 12:6–7). And Solomon says, "For whom the Lord loves He corrects, Just as a father the son in whom he delights" (Prov 3:12). It's as simple as that.

A father does everything in his power to provide his child with guidance and correction; how much more so with God.

God will use trials in our lives to bring about whatever change He feels we need. Trials test our faith, humble us, and are used to further God's plan for us. Look at the words of Paul and Peter:

> And not only that, but we also glory in tribulations, knowing that tribulation produces perseverance; and perseverance, character; and character, hope. (Rom 5:3–4)

> But may the God of all grace, who called us to His eternal glory by Christ Jesus, after you have suffered a while, perfect, establish, strengthen, and settle you. (1 Pet 5:10)

Trials build character—the character traits God, our loving Father, wants for us.

In case the father-child explanation doesn't resonate, God also describes His intention for the trials we face in another way. He compares the work He does in us through trials to the process of refining precious metals. In Psalms, David proclaims, "For You, O God, have tested us; You have refined us as silver is refined" (Ps 66:10). The purpose of metal refining is to remove the impurities within the metal, making the metal much more valuable. The process involves heating the metal to its molten state. Once that happens, the impurities that were trapped within the metal migrate to the surface of the molten mass and become dross as they float on its surface. The dross can then be easily removed, leaving behind the pure metal.

In God's refining process, the refiner's fire pictures the various trials we face in our lives. The dross is whatever character impurities are hiding within the recesses of our hearts that God desires to remove. God may use consequences for our actions to highlight the change in behavior He desires. He may put roadblocks in front of us to move us in a direction we are reluctant or refusing to go. Or He may put something in front of us that we have absolutely no control over to force us to yield our will to His. Whatever the trial is, God uses it to refine us, to purify us, to set us apart, and above all to draw us into a deeper, more intimate relationship with Him.

The book of Job provides us with a complete picture of how God uses the trials of life to develop our character and draw us closer to Him. Job was a man who was "blameless and upright, and one who feared God and shunned evil" (Job 1:1). He was blessed with seven sons and three daughters. His wealth in livestock and servants made him the greatest of all people in the region.

That is, until the day came when God decided to bring a trial into Job's life. God allowed our adversary to attack Job's family and possessions, but he was not allowed to touch Job. As a result of the attack, Job lost all his children and possessions in a single day. Just imagine that—losing all ten children without any warning! All that the Bible tells us about Job's response to this attack is that he mourned for his loss but remained close to God, saying, "Naked I came from my mother's womb, and naked shall I return there. The Lord gave, and the Lord has taken away; blessed be the name of the Lord" (Job 1:21). Obviously, Job's relationship with God was pretty strong when this tragedy occurred, because most of us would struggle to utter these words after such a trial.

But astonishingly, that wasn't the end of the trial. God then allowed Satan to attack Job directly. The only limitation was that he was not allowed to take his life. Job was hit with "painful boils from the sole of his foot to the crown of his head" (Job 2:7). And on top of this, he had to endure pressure from his broken wife, who wanted him to curse God and die, and the criticism and judgment of three of his friends who, instead of comforting him, told him he was obviously doing something wrong and provoking the wrath of God. Even still, though, Job refused to curse God.

However, Job did have character weaknesses buried deep within him, and they started to come to the surface as his pains lingered. He became frustrated and started to question why someone as blameless as him would have to endure such suffering. He questioned God. He wanted answers from God. He wanted to present his case to God so that God would see things from his perspective.

God finally did speak to Job out of a whirlwind, but He did not answer Job's questions the way they were asked. Instead of defending His actions, God questioned Job's wisdom and understanding. How can the creation question anything the Creator does? Then, He gave Job a glimpse of all He does in creating and sustaining all that is. His response to Job demonstrates how intimately involved He is with His creation:

> "Would you indeed annul My judgment?
> Would you condemn Me that you may be justified?
> Have you an arm like God?
> Or can you thunder with a voice like His?
> Then adorn yourself with majesty and splendor,
> And array yourself with glory and beauty.
> Disperse the rage of your wrath;
> Look on everyone who is proud, and humble him.
> Look on everyone who is proud, and bring him low;
> Tread down the wicked in their place.
> Hide them in the dust together,
> Bind their faces in hidden darkness.
> Then I will also confess to you
> That your own right hand can save you." (Job 40:8–14)

God called Job out for questioning His judgments and wanting Him to be condemned so that he would be justified. If Job in all his wisdom and power was able to humble the proud like God, then he should be able to save himself.

Job's response to God's questioning brought about the changes God was looking for in him. Job declares:

> "I know that You can do everything,
> And that no purpose of Yours can be withheld from You.
> You asked, 'Who is this who hides counsel without knowledge?'
> Therefore I have uttered what I did not understand,
> Things too wonderful for me, which I did not know.
> Listen, please, and let me speak;
> You said, 'I will question you, and you shall answer Me.'
> I have heard of You by the hearing of the ear,
> But now my eye sees You.
> Therefore I abhor myself,
> And repent in dust and ashes." (Job 42:2–6)

Job no longer had pride in his goodness. Before his encounter with God, he thought that he knew God, but following it, he realized that God was so much more amazing than he had ever imagined. God honored this transformation in him. In the years that followed, He restored Job's family, giving him seven more sons and three more daughters, and He blessed him with twice the possessions he had before.

There's an interesting sidebar to Job's story that plays into our discussion. It's the question of collateral damage. Job's story is focused on him and his relationship with God, yet Job's ten children and most of his servants were killed. And what about Job's wife? She was affected by this trial almost as much as Job was. Were all these people collateral damage so that God could mold Job's character?

It's an important question that becomes relevant for us as we try to make sense of our own trials. It would absolutely shatter me to think that my beloved son had to endure such pain and suffering because God wanted to cause growth in me!

It is true that others will suffer when trials hit us, so from a physical perspective, there is collateral damage that occurs. The question is, will the negative impact had on others benefit them as well or is there no good that will come from it? For those of us who are followers of God, the answer is summarized very simply by Paul in his letter to the Roman church:

> And we know that God causes all things to work together
> for good to those who love God, to those who are called
> according to His purpose. (Rom 8:28 NASB)

Everything that happens to each and every one of us will ultimately be for our good. That's the completeness of God's work in our lives. We are all connected to each other in so many profound ways.

Don't ever let your mind take you to the place where you feel guilt over the suffering of someone you love. Always remember that God is love. God loves you, and God loves all your loved ones. We are all His children, and we all have our issues. God is working with each and every one of us to mold our characters. So, in my case, I was not the only one who was affected by this trial, and I was not the only one who grew from it. Each person affected had a unique relationship with God, and God had unique areas where He wanted each person to grow.

My life experiences and relationship with God pale in comparison to Job's; however, I've seen significant spiritual growth in my life over the years. The growth never came easily and was never something I would have initiated on my own. It always came through trials, yet there was a confidence always within me that whatever came my way, I had God by my side carrying me through.

Those experiences made it easy for me to connect with Bible passages that show God providing comfort and protection from the evil in this world. There are many, many scriptures like that. Specifically, Psalm 1:3 has provided me with an analogy for spiritual growth that I have meditated on for years. The verse uses a well-watered tree to describe the person who delights in God and meditates on His Word: "He shall be like a tree planted by the rivers of water, that brings forth its fruit in its season, whose leaf also shall not wither; and whatever he does shall prosper" (Ps 1:3).

I think this verse stands out to me because I like trees. Wherever I find myself, I take special notice of them. I am most impressed when I'm in the presence of very old trees. There's a beauty and majesty to them. They tower over everything, and their massive limbs provide support for innumerable leaf-bearing branches that bring welcome shade for the majority of the day and provide a home and food for a wide variety of animals.

When you look closely at old trees, though, you see the damage left behind by limbs that were once a part of their awesome presence and are now gone. Throughout all those seasons of growth, the trees endured many storms that devastated significant portions of them. They, however, lived on and now stand before you the magnificent product of all their life experiences. Had they remained whole, untouched by their environment, their character would not be the same. Their beauty and splendor are so because of the storms they endured, not in spite of them. And so it is with us.

Responding to the Reality

All of this, as each of us who has endured significant trials knows, is easy to say objectively. But made personal—when the storms are our own—the knowledge of trials and their purpose isn't sufficient for lifting our pain. The tree, after all, doesn't admire its own beauty. We need more to help us through. We need God.

I was content with my relationship with God and felt that I could rest in Him and not fear trials. I was good at trusting in God's guidance through trials and resting in the fact that trials would refine my character and draw me into intimacy with Him—that is, when life was good and the trials were bearable. But Daniel's trial blindsided me and knocked me off my foundation.

Like Job, the initial trial rocked me but didn't shake my foundation. I was grounded in God's healing promises and saw God's hand guiding us through Daniel's many treatments. When Daniel was taken, though, my foundation was shaken, and I felt that I had lost my connection with God. There was no joy or peace or taking a broader perspective; there was only pain and hurt and loss. I did not want to be where God had taken me, yet I couldn't change the outcome.

There are passages in the Bible that encourage us to find joy in the trials we face. James says, "My brethren, count it all joy when you fall into various trials, knowing that the testing of your faith produces patience" (Jas 1:2–3). And Peter adds, "Beloved, do not think it strange concerning the fiery trial which is to try you, as though some strange thing happened to you; but rejoice to the extent that you partake of Christ's sufferings, that when His glory is revealed, you may also be glad with exceeding joy" (1 Pet 4:12–13). While it's true that trials are for our good and there will come a time when we will be able to look back on all the trials we faced and see the good, I rejected the notion that I could be joyful as I endured this trial. It just didn't happen.

During Daniel's last weeks, my heart was continuously heavy, and my spirit cried out for direction, comfort, and relief from the pain. There was no enjoyment in eating. It became a chore that I knew needed to be done. I labored to swallow every bite I took. Sleep was not restful. If I woke up for any reason, my mind was immediately drawn to the reality I was fighting to reject, and from that point on, I would not find rest, so I would toss and turn until morning. Every task I performed was difficult. Even the simplest of tasks needed more concentration than I was able to muster. There was no planning of days, or hours, or even minutes. Life was wrapped up in every moment as it came to me.

Every waking thought was toward Daniel's healing, and every moment I was able to sneak away to a quiet place was a time for prayer. Even though I can look back on our experiences and see significant growth in my life, I cannot and probably will not ever view any part of it as joyful. It was hard. It was the hardest time I have ever experienced in my life. I wish I could go back to the time prior to the trial. I would gladly trade any growth to have Daniel back.

My heart cries out for anyone who has to go through a difficult trial. If this is you, you know what I'm talking about. The normal routines of life have suddenly disappeared. You are thrust into this new reality—a reality that you do not want to be a part of at all. As you try to make sense of what's happening, more comes at you. The pain is dull yet constant and overwhelming. No words can bring comfort. The only thing that can bring relief is God taking the trial away from you. So you pray. You pray incessantly. God has taken away all your crutches. You cannot control what's happening. There's no resource or technology or human intervention that will resolve your issue. All that's left is you, standing emotionally naked before your Creator God, wanting desperately for Him to acknowledge your suffering and have compassion on your loved one.

You want desperately for God to provide you with the outcome you desire. You know that there are other outcomes, but you find it hard or impossible to consider them. Even if you pray for God's will to be done, your heart's desire is for the outcome you want. I found that I became so fully vested in Daniel's healing that I made myself believe that God's will for Daniel was healing and that it would come if I stayed in that place. But then, what father wouldn't act that way?

I could easily mask my true feelings because I knew how I should act, but the reality was that I feared even thinking about that loss. So then I buried those thoughts as deeply as I could and snuffed them out anytime they tried to surface. It's like I was trying to hide those feelings from God because I feared that He would bring to reality what I feared the most in order for me to grow. In essence, I was hiding from the loving Father I longed to rest in.

Of course, all of this, we know from the Bible, is not the ideal way to process our trials. In an ideal world, we could see with the eyes of God and fully grasp why, in the big picture of God's story, we should not grieve "like people who have no hope" (1 Thes 4:13 NLT). But in a broken world, we do grieve and lack in faith to fully trust in God.

/ / / /

When faced with trials, we all react differently. We can't anticipate or plan how we will react. Hopefully our suffering will ultimately lead us to God, but we can neither order how that will happen nor do the right thing in every situation. In light of that, we should never allow the opinions of others to cause us to feel shame, and we should never judge others by the words they say or how they react when they're hit with suffering.

Using the example of Job, his friends truly thought they were doing him a service by pointing out the deficiencies they perceived in him. Some of what they said may have been true, but their judgments of Job did not help him and angered God. We all need room to work our way through the trials we face without feeling judged by others. What we need is a compassionate ear, not a critique of how we're acting. When someone is suffering, we can be an immense help to them by coming alongside them, listening to them, and allowing them to express their anger, frustration, confusion, and disappointment. Rather than feel shame for their thoughts, they should feel God's mercy through their interactions with others.

I don't know the trial you're going through. I can't tell you how you should be feeling or acting. Even if you're dealing with the death of a child like I did, your circumstances, point of reference, background, and relationship with God are all different from mine. How you feel and your reaction to what is happening are unique to you and your situation. No one should ever tell you how you should react, and you should never feel judged or shamed by your actions.

We're told that time heals all wounds. I can't tell you how often I heard that comment. It's a well-intended encouragement thought up by sincere people who want to help you get past your mourning or suffering. Yet the implications of this comment are usually not considered by the person giving the advice. Time, in fact, will not heal your loss. The loss will always be there. Time will not heal your anger and hurt. However, it doesn't need to remain. It can change, but change requires action on your part.

The anger I had toward God was directed at His decision to take Daniel home when I wanted Daniel to stay with me. I wanted my way. I came up with solid logic for God answering my prayers for healing, so when God made His decision to take Daniel, I was angry that He didn't agree with me. My desires were understandable. What parent would want anything less than complete healing for their child?

The only way I could break out of my anger was by changing my perspective. The reality of Daniel being gone was not going to change. What had to change was how I internalized what had occurred.

You may feel anger toward God. That anger may be for the same reasons I was angry, or you may have some other issue that you're struggling to let go of. The issues may be different, but the source of the anger is the same. You reject the reality of what happened and feel that God did not answer your prayers in the way you wanted, so there's frustration and anger.

If we don't change our perspective and get over the anger we feel, God's promises for us are just words, and words on their own cannot console the grieving heart. We need to be firmly grounded in what our future holds. When our worldview keeps us focused on this place and time, this physical life we have, it becomes very difficult to move forward.

That brings me to an understanding of trials that I feel compelled to address. It has to do with whether or not God will put a trial before us that we're unable to handle. Will God allow us to experience a trial that destroys us? Our experiences tell us that the answer to this question is yes. We all either know of or have heard of someone who was crushed under the weight of a trial they faced, leading to unresolved anger, a broken family, or even in some cases suicide, all of which seem to lead to separation from the God who put the trial there to bring the individual closer to Him in the first place.

You may be one of these people. You wonder why—*Why did this happen to me? Why did God crush me like this?* Losing Daniel shook me to the core and caused me to be angry with God and question my beliefs. Even though I was not destroyed, I can see how this could happen. I thought

God and I were pretty tight, maybe even to the point of being prideful of my relationship with God. Yet when this trial hit, it threw me for a loop.

The Bible, though, tells us that "No temptation has overtaken you except such as is common to man; but God is faithful, who will not allow you to be tempted beyond what you are able, but with the temptation will also make the way of escape, that you may be able to bear it" (1 Cor 10:13). This verse is talking about temptations, but can we apply this same principle to the trials we face?

When other scriptures are considered in this discussion, we see a similar theme:

> But we have this treasure in earthen vessels, that the excellence of the power may be of God and not of us. We are hard-pressed on every side, yet not crushed; we are perplexed, but not in despair; persecuted, but not forsaken; struck down, but not destroyed. (2 Cor 4:7–9)

> The righteous cry out, and the Lord hears, And delivers them out of all their troubles. The Lord is near to those who have a broken heart, and saves such as have a contrite spirit. (Ps 34:17–18)

Yes, the most difficult trials we face will be more than we can navigate on our own. But the Bible clearly teaches us that God will carry us through all the difficulties of this life, and I believe that's where the answer lies.

As we began to consider previously, we need to take action. We have an adversary who wants nothing more than for us to stay in the place we're at, buried under the weight of our mourning and sorrow, so we can't stay there. Counselors will tell you that you must let go of the reality you can't change and move forward. This is a good message, but it's not the complete answer. On our own, we can't take the necessary steps, so we need God's help.

He is there. He wants to help you. You may never fully understand why God allowed this trial to hit you as it did, but my prayer for you is that you will gain a different perspective on life that gives you hope for the future and peace about what happened. Go to God. Ask Him for the strength to move forward. Ask Him to heal the brokenness of your heart.

Maybe you still have questions, though. Job needed God to answer his questions. I had questions I needed answers for too. After Daniel's passing, I still believed in God. I still believed in His Word. I still believed in His healing for us. And I still believed in prayer. However, I was wounded and needed to know from God, why? It is okay to ask and seek answers to our questions, but ultimately, we all need to come to the place where we trust that God loves us and our loved ones more than we could ever imagine.

When I received no definitive answer, my foundation was still God, but where else could it be? I'm reminded of Paul's defense of the resurrection of Jesus and our hope for the resurrection. He tells us, "If in this life only we have hope in Christ, we are of all men the most pitiable" (1 Cor 15:19). The disciples were confronted with a similar reality. Many had fallen away from Jesus when His doctrine started focusing more on spiritual matters and less on physical healing. Jesus asked His twelve closest disciples if they too wanted to leave, to which Peter replied, "To whom shall we go?" (Jn 6:68). We are angry with God, but that means we believe in God. And our answers can only come from God, so rejecting Him is not the answer.

My hope is in God. My hope for Daniel is in God. I believe and know that Daniel is with God and he will be resurrected to eternal life with our loving Father. This is my hope. Without this hope, I would be lost.

I cannot ignore the reality of what happens to some of us, though. The weight of some trials, maybe yours, is devastating. From all indications, Job's wife was devastated and turned away from God. The only words the Bible records her speaking during their trial were to Job. She said to him, "Do you still hold fast to your integrity? Curse God and die!" (Job 2:9).

Those who, for whatever reason, cannot or will not turn to God in their times of need are not rejected by God. God is still there. God loves you. He loves all of us. Always remember that God is not against us. He has no pleasure in destroying us. He is for us. My worldview leads me to believe that when God's plan for each and every one of us is fulfilled, the trials we faced in our lives will all have worked for our ultimate good and led us to God's eternal destiny for us.

chapter 3

Doesn't God Want to Heal His Children?

The idea of losing a loved one was a thought I never allowed my mind to dwell on. At best, when the topic came up, I would quickly defuse the conversation by saying, "I don't know how anyone could deal with the death of a loved one," shake my head in dismay, and just leave it at that. My faith was not strong enough for me to openly discuss such a tragic event, so I avoided it.

God would not allow me to stay there, though. He took me on a journey that revealed His desire for all of us to be whole, to be healed from all our sicknesses. God illuminated His promises for healing to me through His Word and fulfilled those promises through the healing of Daniel's cancer. But He didn't stop there. He wanted me to know that the fullness of His love for us transcends this time and place. He wanted me to trust that His direction for my son's life was good and perfect.

Before any of Daniel's sicknesses, I would typically pray, asking for healing if God "willed it." I was conditioned to think this way because of what I had been taught and what I had experienced. I knew of God's sovereignty over us, so it became an expression that helped me to package healing in a simple, easy-to-use way, like having a blister packet for processed food. I didn't need to think too deeply about the subject. When someone was in need of healing, I would pray that healing would come if it was God's will. That is, until the healing was needed for someone as closely connected to me as my son. At that point, I knew that an oversimplified expression would not be enough. I needed to know everything God tells us about healing.

So I dove into a study, collecting every scripture I could find on healing. Then I grouped the passages by subtopics or themes. I pored over them and even carried them around with me wherever I went. By doing so, I was able to build a strong foundation that would not be easily shaken.

And that is what I hope for you. I know your fears. I was there—and not all that long ago. So let's walk through this journey together to discover what God has to say about healing.

What Does the Bible Say about Healing?

To start with, it is important to know that when God makes promises to us, He keeps them. Peter tells us, "The Lord is not slack concerning His promise, as some count slackness, but is longsuffering toward us, not willing that any should perish but that all should come to repentance" (2 Pet 3:9).

God makes conditional and unconditional promises in the scriptures. A conditional promise made by God is a promise that God will fulfill once the conditions of the promise are met. These conditions are usually related to God's people being obedient to His commandments. A dad's relationship with his son provides us with countless examples of conditional promises. If dad tells Bubba that he'll buy him a new bike if he improves his grades, Bubba now has a conditional promise from dad. Produce the grades and get the bike. With conditional promises, we have to do our part before God will give us what He promised.

Unconditional promises are promises God makes to us in His grace. We are His children, and He loves us, so when we come to Him in need, He will give us what He has promised with no strings attached. When dad tells Bubba to slow down and taste his food and then reassures him that there will always be food on the table, he's making an unconditional promise to Bubba. No matter how Bubba behaves, dad will always provide food for him to eat.

Old Testament passages conditionally promising healing were given to God's people if they would turn to Him, keep His commandments, serve and please Him, and humble themselves before Him. In the book of Exodus, Moses reminds the Israelites of all the blessings God will pour out on them if they will obey Him.

> If you diligently heed the voice of the Lord your God and do what is right in His sight, give ear to His commandments and keep all His statutes, I will put none of the diseases on you which I have brought on the Egyptians. For I am the Lord who heals you. (Ex 15:26)

Moses told the people that obedience to God would bring His provisions, and a part of those provisions was healing from any sicknesses or diseases. God would remind the people that He, and only He, was their healer. He was teaching His people to come to Him for all their needs, recognize His sovereignty over their lives, obey His commands, and receive all the blessings He would shower upon them.

There are also many Old Testament passages containing unconditional promises for healing. God would make these promises when His people were broken. He would see them cry out to Him and heal them. In one such example from the book of Jeremiah, He says:

> "For I will restore health to you
> And heal you of your wounds," says the Lord,
> "Because they called you an outcast saying:
> 'This is Zion;
> No one seeks her.'" (Jer 30:17)

God promised that He would restore His people's health and heal them from their wounds. He loved His people; they were His children, so He would be there to protect and heal them even when they failed to stay close to Him.

David is a perfect example for us of a man after God's heart, yet even he often fell short of God's desire for him. He writes:

O Lord my God, I cried out to You, and You healed me.
(Ps 30:2)

David knew that God was always there for him, and his experiences with God led him to know that God would heal him when he cried out to Him, regardless of his behavior.

David's walk with God, his experience with God's healing, is a real-life testimony that we can apply to our lives. The Old Testament was not merely given to us as a historical record. It is filled with real people with real issues who found the healing they so desperately needed in the arms of a loving Father God. And further, the Old and New Testaments are perfectly aligned, illuminating the complete picture of God's healing provisions for us.

The solid link between the Old and New Testaments regarding healing came in the person of Jesus, the Anointed One. Several Old Testament scriptures identified the future coming of the Anointed One and the behaviors that would identify Him as such. When Jesus came, He fulfilled all that was said of Him from the Old Testament.

On one occasion, Jesus stood up in the synagogue to read from the book of Isaiah and proceeded to read a prophecy regarding the Chosen One who would come:

"The Spirit of the Lord is upon Me,
Because He has anointed Me
To preach the gospel to the poor;
He has sent Me to heal the brokenhearted,
To proclaim liberty to the captives
And recovery of sight to the blind,
To set at liberty those who are oppressed;
To proclaim the acceptable year of the Lord." (Lk 4:18–19)

Jesus closed the book and, with all eyes on Him, told His audience that He was the fulfillment of those scriptures. It was prophesied that when the Anointed One came, He would heal, and Jesus did just that. Jesus healed.

It's important for us to understand that the Anointed One's mission was not only spiritual healing but physical healing as well. Jesus came to be the healer of our injuries and sicknesses because of His great love for us and to prove that He was the Chosen One—that He was God—the understanding of which was the pathway to both spiritual healing and physical healing.

Bringing physical healing was the way that Jesus would be known to us and assure us of the spiritual healing promised, because physical healing is certainly easier to confirm than spiritual healing. When challenged by the Pharisees on the topic of spiritual healing, the forgiveness of sins, Jesus said:

> "For which is easier, to say, 'Your sins are forgiven you,' or to say, 'Arise and walk'? But that you may know that the Son of Man has power on earth to forgive sins" — then He said to the paralytic, "Arise, take up your bed, and go to your house." And he arose and departed to his house. (Matt 9:5–7)

Forgiveness of sins and miraculous physical healing are both matters that no human can accomplish. Jesus, though, was demonstrating that He had the power to provide both.

Everywhere Jesus went, He healed. People would follow Him. They would travel for miles with their sick just to be able to come into contact with Jesus and be healed. They would line the streets waiting for Him to pass by. They would do whatever it took to get His attention. In one case, the people even resorted to opening up a roof and lowering a sick man to Jesus so that He would heal him (Lk 5:17–26).

He healed lepers, the deaf, the lame, the paralyzed, the demon-possessed, people with various sicknesses, and people near death or dead. He even healed the simplest of sicknesses like a fever. There was no specific method to His healing or requirements for healing. He healed those with faith and those lacking in faith or not demonstrating any faith. He healed those who came to Him and those who were distant. Healing came by touching Jesus or His garment, Jesus laying His hands on the sick, or Jesus simply declaring the healing. What was important was that He was God. He had the power to heal and had compassion on His people. He and only He could make them whole again. Healing was a blessing from God and brought glory to Him.

Imagine what that would have been like, seeing people lining the roadways for miles, waiting for Jesus to pass by. As He would, shouts of joy would ring out as the sicknesses and sufferings of this world were taken away. Imagine if Jesus were walking the earth today and people heard that He was healing any and everyone who came to Him. The mobs of people would be enormous. With the mass media we have today, people from all over the earth would urgently travel to where He was. That's because we all have a fundamental desire for good health, to be whole and live a long, healthy life. The good news for us is that our God still promises that to anyone who comes to Him.

Healing was such an important part of what Jesus was accomplishing here on earth that He gave those same powers to His followers. He sent His twelve closest disciples out to proclaim that His kingdom would soon come, and in doing so gave them power and authority to heal all kinds of sickness and disease as proof of this good news. He said to them:

> "As you go, preach, saying, 'The kingdom of heaven is at hand.' Heal the sick, cleanse the lepers, raise the dead, cast out demons. Freely you have received, freely give." (Matt 10:7–8)

As with Jesus, the disciples' healing power made the people receptive to their message and provided them with the credibility they needed to assure people that they were sent by God.

After they returned, Jesus sent seventy other followers out with the same mission and the same powers to heal (Lk 10:1–9). By sending His followers out in this manner, He was preparing them for what He had in store for them after He left. Jesus told His followers that He was going back to His Father but that He was leaving them with the power to do even greater works than He did (Jn 14:12–14, 16:23–27). He said to ask for such miracles in His name, and they would be done.

There are several examples of healing performed by the disciples of Jesus. In one instance, Peter and John were presented with the opportunity to heal a man as they went to the temple to pray:

And a certain man lame from his mother's womb was carried, whom they laid daily at the gate of the temple which is called Beautiful, to ask alms from those who entered the temple; who, seeing Peter and John about to go into the temple, asked for alms. And fixing his eyes on him, with John, Peter said, "Look at us." So he gave them his attention, expecting to receive something from them. Then Peter said, "Silver and gold I do not have, but what I do have I give you: In the name of Jesus Christ of Nazareth, rise up and walk." And he took him by the right hand and lifted him up, and immediately his feet and ankle bones received strength. So he, leaping up, stood and walked and entered the temple with them—walking, leaping, and praising God. (Act 3:2–8)

This man wasn't expecting healing and didn't exhibit any knowledge of Jesus or faith in Him. He only wanted a handout, yet—without hesitation—Peter healed him. The crowds were all amazed and thought the healing power came from them. Peter, though, recognizing this immediately, pointed them to Jesus, the source of all healing. The power to heal came from God's Spirit, given to the followers of Jesus. And those same powers have been passed on to those of us who have come after, through that same Spirit of God living within us (1 Cor 12:9).

The fact that God gives the gift of healing to some of His followers is important for our discussion, because it illuminates how God works in and through His people to accomplish all He has for His creation. You should always seek out others in the church to pray with you for healing. God has provided many healing angels for you to call on as you navigate through your healing needs.

Always know that any healing comes from God. It is always God's Spirit that provides the healing to us. God may work independent of others or through others. He may work through medical doctors, or medical procedures and methods, or medicines. Whatever the case, all healing is a gift from God and is brought to us by God's Spirit intervening to heal our sicknesses.

Our loving Father wants us to be whole and healthy. When we come to Him, He will heal us. He and only He is our healer. He is there for you. Whatever the sickness is that is standing before you, recognize that God is there with you and wants to be included in your journey.

Prayer

This brings us to another important dimension of healing. God could make healing automatic if that was His desire for us. He could just will healing for us, and it would be done. But that's not God's desire for us. We are His children, and He desires intimacy with us.

Imagine a parent anticipating every desire their child had and providing for those things without any interaction with them and without the child's appreciation for the value of what was provided. What a dysfunctional family. What a dysfunctional relationship between parent and child. The human need for loving interactions between family members would be unfulfilled, and the child would not be driven to grow or mature. It doesn't make any sense, does it?

God wants and wills healing for us, but more importantly, He wants intimacy with us. He wants us to talk to Him. God wants you to include Him in every decision that needs to be made. He wants to direct you to the right doctors, and treatments, and medicines. He wants to draw you to people who will prop you up and give you the spiritual and emotional support you need. He will provide for all your financial concerns if you will only bring them to Him. We call these intimate times spent talking with God prayer. Having knowledge about God's healing power is only beneficial if it leads you to Him, so that's where prayer comes in. Prayer connects us with God.

Over the years, I've seen growth in my prayer life, and no, it didn't come from my graphing fiasco! My prayer life has never been constant. It changes and flows with the trials of life. The purposefulness of my prayers and time spent in prayer is always least when times are good and God is showering me with blessings. I'm sure you can relate to this. The trials of life bring us to our knees, don't they? As I consider the evolution of my prayer life, my first thought always brings me back to a point in time when Daniel was young and immature. He had gotten in with some troubled kids and made some very bad decisions. The consequences of their actions were significant and drove me and Gretchen to our knees, asking for God's intervention and guidance for us and for Daniel.

We decided to write down all of God's promises to our children. Then, each night we would kneel together and pray with the promises laid out before us. We would go through each one, asking God to fulfill that promise in Daniel's life. That was an amazing experience that really deepened our connection with God. It became a turning point in Daniel's life as God carried him through and taught him much-needed life lessons. Since then, Gretchen and I have always prayed together each day, although, as I said, we have not always maintained the same sense of purposefulness.

When Daniel's sicknesses hit, we knew we needed to be firmly rooted in God's promises for healing, and prayer was an integral part of that. Every night, Daniel, Gretchen, and I would spend time together discussing the scriptures I had gathered on healing. Reading through God's promises on healing was a wonderful blessing. Each night, one of us would pick a scripture we liked and read it out loud. We would discuss the meaning of the passage to us and then pray. It really helped Daniel to start verbalizing his inner thoughts.

One night, he actually spoke during the prayer time. This was significant to us because Daniel wasn't confident expressing spiritual matters. We knew that he had a relationship with God, but prior to that, we could only assume how he was internalizing scripture. It brought me back to when he was young and we would pray at bedtime. Daniel was always interested in biblical characters, so he would constantly interrupt stories to ask why. Our hearts' desire was for Daniel's prayers to become heartfelt so that he could open up about his disease and God's promises for him.

It's hard for me to express just how meaningful this time was for us. It was an intimate time spent with God. God gave us peace knowing that He was there for us and spoke to us through each other. Our differing perspectives provided each of us with a well-rounded understanding of His desire for healing.

It was also an intimate time we were given with Daniel. Think about it. How often do we really communicate with our loved ones on an intimate level? How often do we stop the business of life to discuss intimate, personal feelings about our struggles and our relationships with God? How often do we set time aside to give God our undivided attention instead of the micro-prayers we have throughout our days? Yet this is what we were blessed with through this trial. I will always treasure those moments spent together with Daniel and our loving Father. If you take nothing else away from this book, take this! Spend time together in prayer as a family. The blessings you receive will remain with you forever.

Eventually, we reached a point where we had gone through all the scriptures on healing several times. We were at peace with Daniel's situation and confident that God was healing him. We recognized God's love and involvement in his life and had a deepened understanding of God's promises for healing from His Word.

It may be difficult for you to know how to pray. That's okay. Like any relationship worth keeping, getting to a point where conversation is natural, unfiltered, and intimate takes time. New relationships will always include awkward conversation, but you just keep working through it because you're fully vested in making it work. The goal is never to master conversation; it's to have intimacy in your relationship with God.

If you don't pray, I encourage you to get started and not be concerned about how well you're doing. God tells us that His Spirit living within us will intercede on our behalf (Rom 8:26), so even if our words are somewhat misguided, God knows our hearts. The Bible also provides us with countless examples of prayer to guide us in our journey of healing. Jesus Himself provides us with the perfect example of approaching our trials prayerfully.

On one occasion, while Jesus was praying, one of His disciples asked Him to teach them how to pray (Lk 11:1). Jesus used the relationship a father has with his son to explain the mind-set we should have when praying. He explained:

> "So I say to you, ask, and it will be given to you; seek, and you will find; knock, and it will be opened to you. For everyone who asks receives, and he who seeks finds, and to him who knocks it will be opened. If a son asks for bread from any father among you, will he give him a stone? Or if he asks for a fish, will he give him a serpent

instead of a fish? Or if he asks for an egg, will he offer him a scorpion?" (Lk 11:9–12)

While this passage in Luke points directly to the giving of the Holy Spirit, parallel passages guide us to apply this concept more universally. If a father with all his human failings knows how to give his son good things, how much more will God give us when we ask of Him. God wants an intimate relationship with us. He wants us to talk to Him—to let Him know our needs. He wants us to want to seek after Him. And when we do, He will give us more than we ask for. You see, He knows our frame. He knows us better than we know ourselves. He can number the hairs on our head (Matt 10:30), so when we ask Him for help, He doesn't necessarily give us what we want, but He will always give us what we need.

Jesus gave us two simple stories (or parables) to teach us an important lesson about prayer. I clung to the lessons those stories taught me as we navigated through Daniel's sicknesses and our desire for God to heal him.

In the first story, a friend comes to a man's house at midnight asking for food:

> And He said to them, "Which of you shall have a friend, and go to him at midnight and say to him, 'Friend, lend me three loaves; for a friend of mine has come to me on his journey, and I have nothing to set before him'; and he will answer from within and say, 'Do not trouble me; the door is now shut, and my children are with me in bed; I cannot rise and give to you'? I say to you, though he will not rise and give to him because he is his friend, yet because of his persistence he will rise and give him as many as he needs." (Lk 11:5–8)

The man tells his friend to leave because everyone is in bed, but because the friend is persistent and doesn't leave, the man gets up and gives him the bread he is requesting.

In the second story, an unjust judge is initially unwilling to provide justice for a widow:

"There was in a certain city a judge who did not fear God nor regard man. Now there was a widow in that city; and she came to him, saying, 'Get justice for me from my adversary.' And he would not for a while; but afterward he said within himself, 'Though I do not fear God nor regard man, yet because this widow troubles me I will avenge her, lest by her continual coming she weary me.'" Then the Lord said, "Hear what the unjust judge said. And shall God not avenge His own elect who cry out day and night to Him, though He bears long with them? I tell you that He will avenge them speedily." (Lk 18:2–8)

When the unjust judge considered that the woman would not leave him alone until he intervened on her behalf, he was motivated to support her. The lesson with these two parables is that God wants us to be persistent in asking for our desires, to never stop asking until He answers us. No matter what the physical circumstances are or what people are telling you, God wants intimacy with you, so ask!

When the trials of life are bearable, these passages won't stand out to you. It's when the weight of a trial is difficult or impossible for you to bear that you really connect with what Jesus is saying here. You should never feel as though you've already talked to God about your desire so that should be enough. Always remember that God loves you and wants intimacy with you. He wants you to tell Him what's on your heart, so don't ever think that you're bothering Him with your problem.

I spent many, many hours in prayer asking for Daniel's healing. I would think back to these passages and find comfort knowing that God wanted me to keep asking. In a small way, they helped me to more fully know God's character. While it will always be difficult to take my mind back to those times now, I am able to recognize the intimacy I had with our Father and the joy I felt in our victories big and small.

God wants to hear from you. He wants you to talk often to Him. The point isn't to make requests and then sign off. Just think of someone you love very dearly and for some reason are separated from for a long period of time. When you finally get the opportunity to talk on the phone, you don't want the conversations to end. Even if you've already discussed something in the past, you want to hear it again because you just love hearing their voice. And those moments of intimacy you have stay with you forever. That's what God wants. He wants to hear your voice. He wants you to seek after Him and find Him.

There's a passage in the book of James in which James discusses God's desire to bless us with wisdom. He starts off by telling us that God won't withhold wisdom from us if we ask in faith, not doubting. He then goes on to give us good advice about any request we make to God. James tells us that anyone who doubts that they will receive the request they ask for is like a wave being driven and tossed by the wind, that we are double-minded and unstable if we doubt (Jas 1:5–8).

This passage isn't saying that we can demand what we want and expect results or think that the strength of our will causes God to cave in. What it is saying is that we recognize that God is our healer, that He is fully capable of providing healing, that we trust Him to give us what we need, so we ask for healing knowing God wants what's best for us and will never abandon us.

On the night before His death, Jesus spent time in prayer with His Father. He was exceedingly sorrowful, asking for His trial to pass from Him. Yet regardless of what He wanted, He would do the Father's will. It was, in fact, the Father's will that he endure the events to come, so God sent Him an angel to strengthen Him.

Jesus is familiar with the sorrow our trials bring us. He knows that we will want God to take the trials away from us. However, He also knows that God's will is perfect. God did not abandon Him during His difficult time; neither will He abandon us during ours.

What Jesus is teaching here is that it's okay for you to speak what is on your heart. God doesn't want you to tell Him what you think He may want to hear. Remember, He already knows your heart. He wants you to verbalize what's on your heart. You may not have the strength to be at peace with whatever God decides as Jesus was, but that's where you are at this time, so talk to God from that place.

Always know that God is there with you. He hears your pleas. He knows your heart's desires. The time you spend in prayer is very precious to God. Whatever God decides, He is there with you and will never leave you alone.

Character Development

So we see that God does unconditionally promise healing to us. It is ours for the asking. However, our understanding of God's will for healing is not complete yet, because how do we explain the deaths of our loved ones? Despite the unconditional promise for healing available to us, my son Daniel still passed away.

For this, we need to step back a little and remember another promise that the Bible gives us. It says clearly that our petitions will be given to us *when* our requests align with God's will for us:

> Now this is the confidence that we have in Him, that if we ask anything according to His will, He hears us. And if we know that He hears us, whatever we ask, we know that we have the petitions that we have asked of Him. (1 Jn 5:14–15)

We can have complete confidence in receiving what we ask for when our request aligns with God's purpose for us and our loved ones. We've thoroughly discussed God's desire to heal us, so we know God's perspective on that. Yet we are God's children, so God won't always give us what we want but will always give us what we need.

It will always be hard for us to understand the benefit of holding back healing. However, there are a few instances in the Bible when healing did not occur, so let's look at perhaps the most famous of those, in the story of Paul, to help us.

When Paul first encountered Jesus, he was blinded for three days. It wasn't until God sent Ananias to him that his sight was restored (Act 9:8–18). Following this, Paul arguably became the most influential disciple of Jesus, yet even he was denied healing from an infirmity. Paul tells us:

> And lest I should be exalted above measure by the abundance of the revelations, a thorn in the flesh was given to me, a messenger of Satan to buffet me, lest I be exalted above measure. Concerning this thing I pleaded with the Lord three times that it might depart from me. And He said to me, "My grace is sufficient for you, for

My strength is made perfect in weakness." Therefore most gladly I will rather boast in my infirmities, that the power of Christ may rest upon me. (2 Cor 12:7–9)

Paul asked God to heal him three times but was denied because God wanted him to stay humble. God gave Paul extraordinary powers to heal others. Even handkerchiefs or aprons he wore would be brought to the sick and bring healing (Act 9:11–13). This kind of power would quite inevitably lead to pride, so God refused to heal Paul. He wanted Paul to trust that His will for him was sufficient.

Paul was given the insight to know God's will for him. This is likely different from God's will for us, because Paul's walk with God is not the same as our walks with Him. We might never know God's reasons for withholding healing in our own lives. However, we can look at the example of Paul's situation to get a glimpse of God's perspective when the healing doesn't come.

"My grace is sufficient for you," God tells Paul. In all things, God wants us to recognize that He gives life, sustains life, and provides for all our needs. Our part is to turn control of our life over to Him (Jas 4:2–3; 1 Jn 5:14–15). And that's where the rubber meets the road, so to speak. When I first sought to find out what God's Word says about healing, I took all the scriptures we just looked at related to healing and placed them in a tidy little box. I was convinced that all the evidence was there that God wants and wills healing for us. God tells me that He grants every request that aligns with His will, and His will is for healing, so boom! It was a slam dunk that God would heal Daniel!

To be totally transparent, being in the middle of a trial as we were, I don't know if my topical study on healing could ever have been completely objective. I wanted healing for Daniel more than anything else, so that's where I ended up. I wasn't consciously manipulating scripture, but I wasn't able to rise above my biases to let God's Word lead me to the truth. If I could have, I would have found a God who loves Daniel more than I could ever imagine and would be with Daniel and take care of him regardless of whether He healed him or not.

Could any parent who truly loves their child ever want any less than that—for their child to live a full life? Several people would remind me that what happened wasn't natural, that our children should outlive us. I was there. I agreed with that thinking. But life isn't that ordered, and outliving our parents is a luxury we are blessed with in the Western world but is not the standard for most people.

This is a broken world, and God uses the difficulties of life to help us transcend the brokenness—to refine us into versions of ourselves that more closely approach the wholeness that we were originally made for. God is concerned with our character and our connection with Him, so the difficulties of this life are a means to an end. And that means, while it's not what we want to hear in our state of earthly pain, God's ultimate goal is not physical healing, it's spiritual healing.

All too often, we allow the physical constraints of life, the physical laws of nature, to define the extent to which God's power can work in our lives, but Jesus assures us that nothing is impossible for God:

> Jesus looked at them and said to them, "With men this is impossible, but with God all things are possible." (Matt 19:26)

What this is telling us is that God is able to do what He desires. There is nothing that He cannot do. It's easy for us to wrap our minds around this concept when it comes to physical laws. However, when we're faced with seeming contradictions in our convictions, we struggle to accept that God may be bigger than our understanding of Him. We try to put God into a box—a box that fits our understanding and desires. It's understandable why we do this. God tells us:

> "For My thoughts are not your thoughts,
> Nor are your ways My ways," says the Lord.
> "For as the heavens are higher than the earth,
> So are My ways higher than your ways,
> And My thoughts than your thoughts." (Isa 55:8–9)

Since we can never fully understand God, we try to bring Him down to our level of understanding. Yet we're told that God is able to do abundantly more than we can even think to do (Eph 3:20). What we do isn't wrong, but all too often—without realizing it—we come to conclusions about God's will that match our desires, not necessarily His will.

So when we consider that nothing is impossible for God, it's easy for us to apply this truth to healing and say that there's no disease or sickness that God is incapable of healing us from. We know that even death is within His grasp. Yet is it possible for God to withhold healing from us and still be the God who keeps His promises for healing? I really didn't want to explore that question. So when Daniel wasn't healed, I struggled to reconcile how a loving God would allow one of His children to die prematurely. Why didn't God fulfill His promises? At times, I would wrestle with the thought that God was to blame for not doing what He said He would do.

But what if our all-loving God decides that our time on earth is up and He is ready to take us home to Him? Does that make Him a God who doesn't keep His promises, who doesn't heal, or who doesn't love us or our loved ones for whom we are praying for healing?

Someone once put it this way to me: God heals every sickness we have except the last one when we die. In other words, God heals, but He also decides how long we will be here on the earth. At a glance, this adage seems to sum it up, especially for those of us who believe that God is actively healing today. But when you're a parent trying to hold on to any hope of your son being healed, it cuts to the heart.

There's an Old Testament passage that I treasured throughout our journey with Daniel. It speaks of God's love for us and His desire to heal us. I would read the passage, inserting Daniel's name throughout:

> Bless the Lord, O my soul;
> And all that is within me, bless His holy name!
> Bless the Lord, O my soul,
> And forget not all His benefits:
> Who forgives all [Daniel's] iniquities,
> Who heals all [Daniel's] diseases,
> Who redeems [Daniel's] life from destruction,
> Who crowns [Daniel] with lovingkindness and tender mercies,
> Who satisfies [Daniel's] mouth with good things,

So that [Daniel's] youth is renewed like the eagle's. (Ps 103:1–5)

The passage makes a clear distinction between God's promises for spiritual and physical healing, so I trusted that God's plan was to heal Daniel. God, I knew, was sovereign over his life, and that's a wonderful place to be, given the concern and care that God has for His children. God was intimately involved with every step Daniel took, just like a father who watches over and protects his son.

But then Daniel started slipping away. My prayers became more and more urgent, and I perceived that God had turned His back on me. I felt like I couldn't trust Him anymore since He promises healing and yet would not heal Daniel of the heart failure. Was that right thinking, though? Did God turn His back on us, or were the events as they unfolded ordained by God and part of His plan for Daniel's life all along? Was God's care for Daniel as random as it seemed, or was it that I wasn't able to fit what happened into my neat, orderly box of healing?

I couldn't allow myself to believe this because I couldn't let go of control over Daniel's life. You see, if healing was a promise from God that I could identify in His Word and pray for following all the guidelines stated in the Bible, then I could in essence control the situation. I prayed for healing, I prayed expectantly, I prayed continuously, and I prayed in Jesus's name; therefore, I controlled the situation—or at least I thought I did.

When a trial of this magnitude hits you, it's very difficult to be objective. You hold so tightly to every bit of positive information you get from the doctors and compartmentalize the bad or really bad information. I'm sure there's an expert out there who would tell me that this is some type of coping mechanism we use when tragedy strikes. The same thing happened with my understanding of the scriptures on healing, especially after I started my journey of understanding God's will for healing in the midst of Daniel's trial. I held on to every verse that demonstrated that God wanted healing for Daniel and refused to consider that God might have different plans. It was easy for me to reject the notion that God would only heal if it was His will because the Bible provided me with enough evidence to prove that God wanted healing for Daniel.

On top of that, there were many other scriptures that I knew about but ignored for fear of what implications those scriptures would have on my desire for Daniel to be healed. Those scriptures all pointed to God being sovereign over the time we have on this earth. Job 14:5 is one example:

> Since his days are determined,
> The number of his months is with You;
> You have appointed his limits, so that he cannot pass.
> (Job 14:5)

I had no answer for God controlling our length of days here on earth. If God determines our length of days, then there was nothing I could do to intervene. I would have to trust in God. I would have to trust that His plan for Daniel was good, that He had Daniel's best interests in mind, that He loved Daniel and would take care of him. I would have to let go of any control I thought I had and rely solely on our loving God and rest in His will for Daniel's life.

At the time, I couldn't do that, so God took away any crutch that I had and told me to step out onto the waves as they crashed against me and walk toward Him, keeping my eyes focused on Him alone. That was so difficult. I was afraid to take a step. I kept looking at my potential loss and how it would affect Daniel. It made me realize that my faith wasn't as strong as I thought it was. I had talked myself into believing that if I held onto God's promises for healing and didn't waver, I was being faithful. But in reality, I was unwilling to look at all God has for us, rest in God's love for Daniel, and trust that whether or not healing came, Daniel would be okay because he is God's child and God loves him more than I ever could.

To move forward and understand the fullness of God's love and care for your loved one, you need to follow me on this next step of the journey. While I wasn't willing to acknowledge these amazing scriptures during Daniel's trial, I will tell you that they hold the key to finding true peace in whatever your situation is. So let's do this together.

God blesses us with a spirit that makes us who we are and connects us to Him:

"But there is a spirit in man,
And the breath of the Almighty gives him understanding."
(Job 32:8)

.While we look at death as the end of life, God views it as the time our spirit finally returns to Him:

Then the dust will return to the earth as it was,
And the spirit will return to God who gave it. (Eccl 12:7)

God gives us our spirit when we are created. It's our spirit that makes us in God's image. When we breathe our last breath, our spirit returns home to our Father.

There are two passages in which God illuminates for us just how important the end of our time on earth is to Him:

Precious in the sight of the Lord is the death of His saints.
(Ps 116:15)

A good name is better than precious ointment,
And the day of death than the day of one's birth. (Eccl 7:1)

God views death so differently than we do. The time of death may be tragic for loved ones, but it is a special, precious time to God. Oh, if we could only hold on to the magnitude of what God is teaching us here! God's words tell us that death is not the end; it's the beginning of a new relationship, a more intimate relationship with our Father. Our spirit returns to God, and that is a very precious time to Him.

God tells us that it is He who determines how long we will live on the earth. His plan for each of us is a perfect plan. God accomplishes all He has planned for us in the time He's allotted for us, and He then takes us home.

But God's sovereignty over our lives does not only extend to how long we will live; God is intimately involved in every step we take (Isa 46:9–10), so much so that He knows the number of hairs on our heads (Matt 10:30). As Paul declared the existence of our Creator God to the educated men of Athens, he said:

Nor is He worshiped with men's hands, as though He needed anything, since He gives to all life, breath, and all things. And He has made from one blood every nation of men to dwell on all the face of the earth, and has determined their preappointed times and the boundaries of their dwellings, so that they should seek the Lord, in the hope that they might grope for Him and find Him, though He is not far from each one of us. (Act 17:25–27)

For each and every one of us, God determined at what point in history He would bring us into the world. He decided what part of the world we would live in and who our parents would be. David acknowledged this, saying to God:

My frame was not hidden from You,
When I was made in secret,
And skillfully wrought in the lowest parts of the earth.
Your eyes saw my substance, being yet unformed.
And in Your book they all were written,
The days fashioned for me,
When as yet there were none of them. (Ps 139:15–16)

From even before we were born, God knew what His plan for each of us would be. He had already written our story in His book of life. He skillfully and purposefully made us. Our story contains all the days He fashioned and prepared for us. And with this plan, God causes all things to work together for our ultimate good so that His purposes for us will be fulfilled. God fashions each of our hearts individually.

And we know that all things work together for good to those who love God, to those who are the called according to His purpose. (Rom 8:28)

The Lord looks from heaven;
He sees all the sons of men.
From the place of His dwelling He looks
On all the inhabitants of the earth;

He fashions their hearts individually;
He considers all their works. (Ps 33:13–15)

There is no one plan or approach that God uses for His children. The gifts we're born with, the blessings we're given, the events that unfold before us, and the trials we face are all determined by God and are unique to each of us.

For all believers alike, though, God assures us that we break free of the bondage of death (Heb 2:15) and enter into His peace (Isa 57:1–2) when we leave this earth. And He reminds us through David that being in His presence is better than this temporary life we have: "Because Your lovingkindness is better than life, my lips shall praise You" (Ps 63:3).

Do you see where God is taking us? My perspective was so different from how God views things. The reason I became lost and confused was because I refused to see the fullness of God's plan for us and viewed healing only through the lens of here and now, this physical life we live. I thought that this life was more precious than the life that God intended for us all along. I was so caught up in preserving Daniel's physical life I couldn't see that I was trying to hold him back from so much more.

The life we live here on earth is short and full of blessings and trials that work together to shape our character and prepare us for our amazing next step as God welcomes us home. He set a plan in motion for our lives long before we were born, and He is intimately involved in every step we take in this life, using the blessings and difficulties of this life to mold us. When His plan has reached its fullness, God will take us back into His loving arms where we belong.

God's Healing Summarized

I realize that as my walk with our Creator continues to mature, my perspective will continue to evolve too. So then, here's what God has given me up to this point. Let me start by saying that there is no recipe or ordered steps to take to ensure healing. We cannot use God's Word as a way to control the outcomes we desire. I made that mistake. My purpose in summarizing what I've learned about healing is to give you a broad perspective on God's desire for your life and to guide you through your trials.

44

God's healing of His people was a common theme of the Old Testament. The link between the Old and New Testaments regarding healing came in the person of Jesus, the Anointed One. When Jesus came, He fulfilled all that was said of Him from the Old Testament. Jesus healed everyone He came into contact with needing healing. There was no specific method to His healing or requirement for healing. What was important was that He was God. He had the power to heal and had compassion for His people. He and only He could make them whole again. Healing was a blessing from God and brought glory to Him.

God is our healer. He will bring healing to us though His followers, through aprons, through doctors, through medicine, or through miracles. It doesn't matter how the healing comes, but when it does come, always know that it came from God.

God wants an intimate relationship with us. He wants us to talk to Him, to let Him know our needs. He wants us to want to seek after Him. When we do, He will give us more than we ask for. He knows our frame. He knows us better than we know ourselves. He can number the hairs on our head, so He knows what's best for us. God wants us to be persistent in asking for our desires, to never stop asking until He answers us. And God will answer us. No matter what the physical circumstances are or what people are telling you, God wants intimacy with you, so ask, ask, ask!

God doesn't promise that He will give us anything that our hearts desire or imagine. Rather, He promises to hear and give us what we ask for when it aligns with His will. God does want for us to be whole, to be healed, to be complete in Him. He also wants us to recognize that He gives life, sustains life, and provides for all our needs. Our part is to turn control of our lives over to Him.

This is a broken world, so God uses the difficulties of life to refine us. God may not give us what we ask for, but He will always give us what we need. That means that there are times when more can be gained in the absence of healing. We are to pray to God and rest in God, and He will give us peace and lift us up.

We should never doubt that we will receive what we ask for. Acting that way is like being "a wave being driven and tossed by the wind" (Jas 1:6). We recognize that God is our healer, capable of healing all ailments, and trust that He will give us what we need, so we ask for healing confidently.

God determines how long we will live on this earth. He determines when we will be born and when we will die. Not only that, as He orders our days, He causes all things to work together for our ultimate good so that His purposes for us will be fulfilled. God fashions each of our hearts individually. The time of someone's death to God is a wonderfully intimate time for both God and His child. We are released from the bondage of death and enter into His peace when we leave this earth.

As God has carried me through this difficult trial, I have gained a much more mature understanding of His plan for us and His love for us. All of those things I learned about God's healing as we journeyed with Him through Daniel's sicknesses were true—every single one of them. I just needed to learn to let go and trust God, to stop trying to control Him by putting Him in a box that matched my needs and expectations.

So then, where does this leave you? Should you pray for healing? Absolutely yes! That is God's desire for you. I can't imagine how anyone would be able to navigate intense trials on their own without including God in their journey. I would have fallen apart like a cheap suit had it not been for God providing me with the strength, courage, and wisdom to move forward.

You need God in your life. You need Him for every step you take navigating the trials of your life. He is our healer, so if healing comes, it will come from Him and Him alone. So pray for healing. Pray for God to strengthen everyone connected to your trial. Pray for guidance in all the decisions you will need to make. Ask God to open doors that clarify the path He has chosen for you and to close doors He doesn't want you walking through.

Talk to Him about your desires and weaknesses and fears. Ask Him for the strength to endure every setback you encounter. Don't try to hide anything you're feeling from Him. Take all the raw emotions you have to Him.

And finally, let God know of your worst fears and your reluctance to accept His plan for you or your loved one regardless of the outcome. Ask Him to bless you with the faith to trust that His direction is only good and perfect.

When God *Does* Heal

When you lose a loved one, it's hard to see anything but loss. It was hard for me, as I've said, to think anything but that God didn't keep His promise to heal Daniel. But Daniel's story testifies of God's healing power.

As you may recall from his story, in 2017 we were given the wonderful news that Daniel had no trace of the CLL in his bone marrow, his blood counts were back to normal levels, and his lymph nodes were no longer swollen. He was healed, and this despite the grim prognosis that had come at the beginning of his sickness. Following this, Daniel was given six months of freedom. The chemo was done, the cancer was gone, and we were looking forward to closing out the final months of treatment and putting this chapter of Daniel's life behind us. Our hearts were so thankful to God, yet we didn't feel an overwhelming sense of joy over the news. We felt peace, like God was following through on His promises for Daniel, and this was just another indication that He was there with us. Peace.

Through this chapter, I've given you a complete picture of what my family learned from God as He blessed us with glimpses of His will for us. Yet it's important we don't lose sight of the wonderful gift of healing He brought to Daniel and blessed us with.

As we journeyed with God through Daniel's treatments for the CLL, it was clear to us that God wanted healing for Daniel and God was healing him. There was a peace and confidence there. We were firmly established in God's healing promises and felt God's presence with us as countless doors were opened for us and we were given access to wonderful people and institutions. We saw God's hand in every step we took.

Our journey brought us the joys of being in close intimacy with God as He healed Daniel and the anger and confusion and sense of abandonment as God decided to take Daniel home. Yet God didn't change. He was always there. He will always be there.

chapter 4

God's Comforting Promises

In this chapter, I want to provide you with all the verses that were so important to me as we made our way through Daniel's sicknesses. Use them. Read them often. Consider them in your prayers to God and in the meditations of your day. They will bring you comfort and intimacy with God.

Healing

I shared with you previously that after Daniel was diagnosed with CLL, he, Gretchen, and I would spend an hour every night reviewing scriptures on healing. The following are the Old Testament promises we came to love. They gave us comfort and confidence in God's healing power.

> Bless the Lord, O my soul;
> And all that is within me, bless His holy name!
> Bless the Lord, O my soul,
> And forget not all His benefits:
> Who forgives all your iniquities,
> Who heals all your diseases,
> Who redeems your life from destruction,
> Who crowns you with lovingkindness and tender mercies,
> Who satisfies your mouth with good things,

So that your youth is renewed like the eagle's. (Ps 103:1–5)

"Blessed be the Lord, who has given rest to His people Israel, according to all that He promised. There has not failed one word of all His good promise, which He promised through His servant Moses." (1 Kgs 8:56)

O Lord my God, I cried out to You,
And You healed me. (Ps 30:2)

Then they cried out to the Lord in their trouble,
And He saved them out of their distresses.
He sent His word and healed them,
And delivered them from their destructions.
Oh, that men would give thanks to the Lord for His goodness,
And for His wonderful works to the children of men! (Ps 107:19–21)

He heals the brokenhearted and binds up their wounds. (Ps 147:3)

When you have a loved one in need of healing, reading Bible passages that show the compassion Jesus has for sick and suffering people brings comfort. As I read through the accounts of healing performed by Jesus, I found the confidence to stand firm in my belief that God wills healing for us because Jesus healed every single person He came into contact with needing healing. The passages provided here are unique experiences Jesus had on His journeys, demonstrating this profound truth.

When the men had come to Him, they said, "John the Baptist has sent us to You, saying, 'Are You the Coming One, or do we look for another?'" And that very hour He cured many of infirmities, afflictions, and evil spirits; and to many blind He gave sight. Jesus answered and said to them, "Go and tell John the things you have seen and heard: that the blind see, the lame walk, the lepers are cleansed, the deaf hear, the dead are raised, the poor have the gospel preached to them." (Lk 7:20–22)

Then Jesus went about all the cities and villages, teaching in their synagogues, preaching the gospel of the kingdom, and healing every sickness and every disease among the people. (Matt 9:35)

Jesus departed from there, skirted the Sea of Galilee, and went up on the mountain and sat down there. Then great multitudes came to Him, having with them the lame, blind, mute, maimed, and many others; and they laid them down at Jesus' feet, and He healed them. So the multitude marveled when they saw the mute speaking, the maimed made whole, the lame walking, and the blind seeing; and they glorified the God of Israel. (Matt 15:29–31)

Wherever He entered, into villages, cities, or the country, they laid the sick in the marketplaces, and begged Him that they might just touch the hem of His garment. And as many as touched Him were made well. (Mk 6:56)

When the sun was setting, all those who had any that were sick with various diseases brought them to Him; and He laid His hands on every one of them and healed them. (Lk 4:40)

Faith in Healing

We were continually faced with people, events, and situations that worked to shake our faith in God's ability and desire to bring healing to Daniel. Whenever these attacks surfaced, I would go to passages that reminded me of God's power over His creation. I found strength when I was reminded that nothing is impossible for God, so I just needed to trust in Him, for He was my strength.

Trust in the Lord with all your heart, and lean not on your own understanding; In all your ways acknowledge Him, and He shall direct your paths. Do not be wise in your own eyes; Fear the Lord and depart from evil. It will be health to your flesh, and strength to your bones. (Prov 3:5–8)

But Jesus looked at them and said to them, "With men this is impossible, but with God all things are possible." (Matt 19:26)

So Jesus answered and said to them, "Have faith in God. For assuredly, I say to you, whoever says to this mountain, 'Be removed and be cast into the sea,' and does not doubt in his heart, but believes that those things he says will be done, he will have whatever he says. Therefore I say to you, whatever things you ask when you pray, believe that you receive them, and you will have them." (Mk 11:22–24)

And He said to me, "My grace is sufficient for you, for My strength is made perfect in weakness." Therefore most gladly I will rather boast in my infirmities, that the power of Christ may rest upon me. (2 Cor 12:9)

God Fashions Our Days

Once I realized that God views death much differently than we do, I dug deeper into His Word to understand all He has in store for us. Just knowing that God directs all our paths and determines our time on this earth gave me comfort.

> Precious in the sight of the Lord
> Is the death of His saints. (Ps 116:15)

> A good name is better than precious ointment,
> And the day of death than the day of one's birth. (Eccl 7:1)

My frame was not hidden from You,
When I was made in secret,
And skillfully wrought in the lowest parts of the earth.
Your eyes saw my substance, being yet unformed.
And in Your book they all were written,
The days fashioned for me,
When as yet there were none of them. (Ps 139:15–16)

The Lord looks from heaven;
He sees all the sons of men.
From the place of His dwelling He looks
On all the inhabitants of the earth;
He fashions their hearts individually;
He considers all their works. (Ps 33:13–15)

Prayer

The following passages provided me and Gretchen with a framework for our prayers for healing. We would frequently pray together, confidently asking God for Daniel's healing.

Now this is the confidence that we have in Him, that if we ask anything according to His will, He hears us. And if we know that He hears us, whatever we ask, we know that we have the petitions that we have asked of Him. (1 Jn 5:14–15)

"Again I say to you that if two of you agree on earth concerning anything that they ask, it will be done for them by My Father in heaven. For where two or three are gathered together in My name, I am there in the midst of them." (Matt 18:19–20)

"So I say to you, ask, and it will be given to you; seek, and you will find; knock, and it will be opened to you. For everyone who asks receives, and he who seeks finds, and to him who knocks it will be opened. If a son asks for bread from any father among you, will he give him a stone? Or if he asks for a fish, will he give him a serpent instead of a fish? Or if he asks for an egg, will he offer him a scorpion?" (Lk 11:9–12)

And He said to them, "Which of you shall have a friend, and go to him at midnight and say to him, 'Friend, lend me three loaves; for a friend of mine has come to me on his journey, and I have nothing to set before him'; and he will answer from within and say, 'Do not trouble me; the door is now shut, and my children are with me in bed; I cannot rise and give to you'? I say to you, though he will not rise and give to him because he is his friend, yet because of his persistence he will rise and give him as many as he needs." (Lk 11:5–8)

Now to Him who is able to do exceedingly abundantly above all that we ask or think, according to the power that works in us, to Him be glory in the church by Christ Jesus to all generations, forever and ever. Amen. (Eph 3:20–21)

Be anxious for nothing, but in everything by prayer and supplication, with thanksgiving, let your requests be made known to God; and the peace of God, which surpasses all understanding, will guard your hearts and minds through Christ Jesus. (Phil 4:6–7)

God's Promises to Our Children

When our boys would get into trouble or experience trials of their own, Gretchen and I would kneel together and recite these verses, asking God to fulfill His promises for our children and help them through their difficulties. This became a pattern for us in our prayer life that helped us through the most difficult times.

All your children shall be taught by the Lord,
And great shall be the peace of your children. (Isa 54:13)

Then Peter said to them, "Repent, and let every one of you
be baptized in the name of Jesus Christ for the remission
of sins; and you shall receive the gift of the Holy Spirit.
For the promise is to you and to your children, and to all
who are afar off, as many as the Lord our God will call."
(Act 2:38–39)

So they said, "Believe on the Lord Jesus Christ, and you
will be saved, you and your household." (Act 16:31)

The Lord is not slack concerning His promise, as some
count slackness, but is longsuffering toward us, not
willing that any should perish but that all should come to
repentance. (2 Pet 3:9)

God's Love

God's love was expressed to me throughout my life, yet I lost sight of it
when Daniel left us. While these passages do not reflect all the dimensions
of God's love, they were pivotal in re-grounding my thinking and helping
me to see God's love all around me.

He who does not love does not know God, for God is
love. (1 Jn 4:8)

"For God so loved the world that He gave His only
begotten Son, that whoever believes in Him should not
perish but have everlasting life." (Jn 3:16)

"This is My commandment, that you love one another as
I have loved you. Greater love has no one than this, than
to lay down one's life for his friends. You are My friends
if you do whatever I command you. No longer do I call
you servants, for a servant does not know what his master

54

is doing; but I have called you friends, for all things that I heard from My Father I have made known to you. You did not choose Me, but I chose you and appointed you that you should go and bear fruit, and that your fruit should remain, that whatever you ask the Father in My name He may give you. These things I command you, that you love one another." (Jn 15:12–17)

Love suffers long and is kind; love does not envy; love does not parade itself, is not puffed up; does not behave rudely, does not seek its own, is not provoked, thinks no evil; does not rejoice in iniquity, but rejoices in the truth; bears all things, believes all things, hopes all things, endures all things. (1 Cor 13:4–7)

And now abide faith, hope, love, these three; but the greatest of these is love. (1 Cor 13:13)

God's Family

As I struggled to know that Daniel was being cared for through his sickness and after he left this world, the realization that he is a child of God helped me to find peace in letting go of him. God is our Father, and we are His children. How can I ever doubt God's care for Daniel knowing that Daniel is His child?

> The Lord is my shepherd;
> I shall not want.
> He makes me to lie down in green pastures;
> He leads me beside the still waters.
> He restores my soul;
> He leads me in the paths of righteousness
> For His name's sake.
> Yea, though I walk through the valley of the shadow of death,
> I will fear no evil;

For You are with me;
Your rod and Your staff, they comfort me.
You prepare a table before me in the presence of my
enemies;
You anoint my head with oil;
My cup runs over.
Surely goodness and mercy shall follow me
All the days of my life;
And I will dwell in the house of the Lord
Forever. (Ps 23)

And because you are sons, God has sent forth the Spirit
of His Son into your hearts, crying out, "Abba, Father!"
Therefore you are no longer a slave but a son, and if a son,
then an heir of God through Christ. (Gal 4:6–7)

Grace and peace be multiplied to you in the knowledge
of God and of Jesus our Lord, as His divine power has
given to us all things that pertain to life and godliness,
through the knowledge of Him who called us by glory
and virtue, by which have been given to us exceedingly
great and precious promises, that through these you may
be partakers of the divine nature, having escaped the
corruption that is in the world through lust. (2 Pet 1:2–4)

for in Him we live and move and have our being, as also
some of your own poets have said, "For we are also His
offspring." Therefore, since we are the offspring of God,
we ought not to think that the Divine Nature is like gold
or silver or stone, something shaped by art and man's
devising. (Act 17:28–29)

Behold what manner of love the Father has bestowed on
us, that we should be called children of God! Therefore
the world does not know us, because it did not know Him.
Beloved, now we are children of God; and it has not yet

been revealed what we shall be, but we know that when He is revealed, we shall be like Him, for we shall see Him as He is. And everyone who has this hope in Him purifies himself, just as He is pure. (1 Jn 3:1–3)

For I consider that the sufferings of this present time are not worthy to be compared with the glory which shall be revealed in us. For the earnest expectation of the creation eagerly waits for the revealing of the sons of God. For the creation was subjected to futility, not willingly, but because of Him who subjected it in hope; because the creation itself also will be delivered from the bondage of corruption into the glorious liberty of the children of God. (Rom 8:18–21)

Trials

I wasn't able to find any comfort from passages that told me there was a higher purpose that God was accomplishing in us through Daniel's trial. I would have gladly given up any sort of growth for Daniel's healing. However, just knowing that God was there with me carrying me through brought peace to me.

But may the God of all grace, who called us to His eternal glory by Christ Jesus, after you have suffered a while, perfect, establish, strengthen, and settle you. (1 Pet 5:10)

But we have this treasure in earthen vessels, that the excellence of the power may be of God and not of us. We are hard-pressed on every side, yet not crushed; we are perplexed, but not in despair; persecuted, but not forsaken; struck down, but not destroyed (2 Cor 4:7–9)

The righteous cry out, and the Lord hears,
And delivers them out of all their troubles.
The Lord is near to those who have a broken heart,

And saves such as have a contrite spirit.
Many are the afflictions of the righteous,
But the Lord delivers him out of them all. (Ps 34:17–19)

Yet in all these things we are more than conquerors through Him who loved us. For I am persuaded that neither death nor life, nor angels nor principalities nor powers, nor things present nor things to come, nor height nor depth, nor any other created thing, shall be able to separate us from the love of God which is in Christ Jesus our Lord. (Rom 8:37–39)

"Come to Me, all you who labor and are heavy laden, and I will give you rest. Take My yoke upon you and learn from Me, for I am gentle and lowly in heart, and you will find rest for your souls. For My yoke is easy and My burden is light." (Matt 11:28–30)

Comfort

There are so many passages in the scriptures that talk of God's desire to comfort and protect us. I wasn't looking for assurance of God's comfort throughout Daniel's trials because I was resting in the knowledge that God was healing him. Once Daniel was taken, though, the grief made me lose sight of God's presence with me. I felt that He had abandoned me. These passages helped me to know that God was there with me and would never leave my side.

"Blessed are those who mourn,
For they shall be comforted." (Matt 5:4)

Blessed be the God and Father of our Lord Jesus Christ, the Father of mercies and God of all comfort, who comforts us in all our tribulation, that we may be able to comfort those who are in any trouble, with the comfort with which we ourselves are comforted by God. (2 Cor 1:3–4)

"For I know the thoughts that I think toward you, says the Lord, thoughts of peace and not of evil, to give you a future and a hope. Then you will call upon Me and go and pray to Me, and I will listen to you. And you will seek Me and find Me, when you search for Me with all your heart." (Jer 29:11–13)

The Lord your God in your midst, the Mighty One, will save; He will rejoice over you with gladness, He will quiet you with His love, He will rejoice over you with singing. (Zeph 3:17)

"Fear not, for I am with you; Be not dismayed, for I am your God. I will strengthen you, yes, I will help you, I will uphold you with My righteous right hand." (Isa 41:10)

The Lord is my strength and my shield; My heart trusted in Him, and I am helped; Therefore my heart greatly rejoices, and with my song I will praise Him. (Ps 28:7)

chapter 5

A Journey of Faith

Have you ever been to the ocean and played in the waves? The waves come in continuously and can get pretty powerful, so you have to turn your body and brace yourself as they roll past you. If you get distracted or aren't properly positioned, the waves will knock you off your feet and send you tossing, tumbling, and finally crashing into the beach. Hopefully the experience won't leave you too injured. It will certainly, however, leave you with sand in the most interesting places.

Isn't that how faith works? The trials of life continually crash against you. Your faith positions you to endure the waves that are trying to knock you off your foundation. There are times when we are firmly rooted in the promises of God, so we're unshakeable as we see the trials of life approaching. Yet there are other times, usually when life is good, when we're hit by a wave that knocks us down. When this happens, our connection with God is temporarily lost as we're caught up in our misery.

Throughout Daniel's sickness, my journey of faith was continually being tested. There were times when I was positioned for the attacks, and there were times when the attacks swept me away. Daniel's passing was one such wave—the biggest of all—that swept me away. And when he passed away, it wasn't only him, my beloved son, that I lost; I lost my connection with my beloved Father too. That realization left me feeling empty and betrayed.

My journey isn't your journey. The circumstances will be different.

The waves that crash into you will be unique to your situation, and the waves that knock you down will not be the same as the waves that got to me. Yet our journey is the same. We are all hit with issues we stand against and issues that knock us down. We all have moments of tremendous intimacy with God and times when we feel abandoned and betrayed.

Our journey of faith isn't easy, but the rewards are very special. Allow me to share my journey with you so that together we can use the faith that God gives us to maybe not move mountains but at least endure the waves that knock us down and minimize the sand in our shorts.

The Testing of Faith

From the time of Daniel's CLL diagnosis, it was a struggle for me to keep my eyes on God and not despair. Even when I would talk to people about Daniel's sickness, verbalizing what he had would bring me down. It was like the sickness had taken away my will to move forward. I soon realized that I was submitting to the disease. The disease had power over me. It took away my joy, any sense of normalcy, and was working to take away my hope.

God strengthened my faith by illuminating His Word to me and guiding me back to it every time I faced a spiritual attack. And once God saw the growth in my faith, He brought healing to Daniel. He took away the blood clotting issues and then the cancer.

I saw His hand work through all the details. From the identification of where to go for treatment, to the kindness and compassion of the doctors, to the insurance coverage and support from Daniel's work for the trips, to financial provision for all the travel involved, to opening up a clinical trial that was a perfect fit for Daniel, to healing Daniel, God's presence was there with us and very evident to me. Then Daniel was cancer-free, and I was at peace.

But God wasn't done with me yet. God wanted me to go to a place that I was unwilling to go. This testing of my faith was intense and continuous. It started off when the doctors were telling us that Daniel had heart failure and an inguinal hernia. The shock of what I was being told immediately put me in a fog again. I prayed for understanding and concluded that our adversary was attacking Daniel and us. He was trying to turn us from God. This conclusion gave me marching orders; it was something I could control. If my adversary was attacking us, then I needed to become stronger in my convictions, so that's what I did. I pulled the family together to pray that God would protect us from these attacks, help us to keep our eyes on Him, and bring complete healing to Daniel, just as He had done in the past.

Changes in Daniel's condition, however, were unfolding rapidly, so there was little time for reflection. I was put in a mode of continually reacting to what was in front of me. It's hard for me to describe how I was feeling when we met up with Sarah at the emergency room and she warned us of what we were walking into, then when the doctors told us Daniel was in grave condition and emergency room staff intensely worked to save his life. It all happened so quickly. Keeping my eyes on God? There was none of that now. To consciously think about anything other than what was unfolding before me was impossible. I would have micro-prayers when my mind could focus, but for the most part, I was just reacting to what happened next.

We all believed that the six months that Daniel was free from the CLL were the result of God's healing and an indication that God wanted Daniel to live a full life, so Gretchen and I believed and trusted that God was going to heal Daniel again. Whether healing came through drugs, or a new heart, or God's direct intervention wasn't for us to concern ourselves with. God was in control. God's will for Daniel was his healing, we knew, so He would work that out in His way and His timing. Our part was to believe and trust, so we did.

Even as the doctors were telling us that a large part of Daniel's brain had died, I was calm and had the thought, *Okay, God, the stage is set for You to be glorified through the healing of Daniel.* But that healing never came. I kept hoping that God would bring Daniel back, but his lifeless body lay there for seven more hours connected to life support as family members made their way to the hospital to say their last goodbyes to him. God never intervened, so Daniel's body died shortly after the life support was disconnected.

In the following minutes, hours, and days, I perceived that God had turned His back on Daniel. The feelings that God had rejected us were very, very strong. I thought God loved me. I thought God loved Daniel.

I had, as you already know, spent countless hours studying scriptures on healing. And after all that time, the conclusions I reached caused me to believe that God wanted and willed healing for Daniel and that He wanted me to pray like it had already happened and to pray often for what my heart's desire was.

I witnessed God's healing once, but then Daniel wasn't healed in the end, so all of my past experiences were wiped away as if I had believed in a lie. Over and over again, questions came to mind, and each time, the question was different. *What am I to think about God's Word? Do I have the ability as a human to truly understand God's will and direction for us? How can I believe and hope for any of God's promises in the Bible if He breaks His promises for healing? How can I ever trust God Himself again?* Those thoughts left me feeling empty and betrayed.

I felt like all my previous desire to know and follow God's will was empty and useless because I wasn't able to make sense of what had happened to Daniel through scripture. For a period of time, when I would hear scriptures discussed or their meaning debated, I couldn't help but think how vain the endeavor was. Why study scripture? Why should we try to understand God's will? Isn't it all meaningless and vanity if God's will and His mind are so much higher than ours and His thoughts so high above ours? Isaiah tells us that God's thoughts and ways are higher than we could ever achieve (Isa 55:8–9). So then what's the use?

And what of prayer? During the last two weeks at the hospital, I was in prayer continuously for Daniel's healing, but I have to say that it felt one-sided, like I was doing all the praying, but God wasn't listening. He certainly wasn't responding. Daniel wasn't healed. I never felt comforted or felt God's presence during that entire period. It was as if God had already made His decision, so anything I asked for was ignored. I had never felt so spiritually empty and alone.

At the time, I couldn't help but think that I had done something wrong, so God was punishing me, or that the way I was approaching God in prayer was incorrect, so my prayers were being ignored. I would pray for God's intervention. Then I would think that I was forgetting to ask in Jesus's name, so then I would focus on saying "In Jesus's name" with every request. Then the thought would occur to me that I wasn't asking enough, so I started spending more time in prayer until just about every waking hour was consumed with prayer. Still nothing. Was it my pride or lust or selfishness causing God to turn away? Was it that I was arrogant thinking that I knew God's will for Daniel?

I was trapped in this internal struggle, yet my heart's desire was for Daniel's healing, so I ceaselessly went to God asking for forgiveness for my sins, forgiveness for my selfishness and inability to pray appropriately—"only please, God, let Daniel be healed." But even then, still nothing. Daniel's health continued to slip away, and I wasn't feeling God's presence with us.

I started asking God to give me a sign and show me He was there. Was it wrong to ask for a sign from God? Was it wrong to desire to hear from God? Was it wrong that I needed some feeling of comfort? Was it wrong to not rest in God's Word alone? I prayed and believed and trusted, but I was internally tormented by this sense of inadequacy and guilt and feeling that God wasn't listening.

I knew that there was emptiness there, that I wasn't feeling God's presence or peace with me. I was afraid to dwell on that feeling because I wanted to stay focused on healing for Daniel, but I found myself quite frequently asking for God to reveal Himself to me, or speak to me, or speak to me through someone else. It's as if my spirit knew that God was distant from me for some reason and was reaching out to Him for help, yet I wouldn't consciously admit that this was happening and that this was what I was doing. It wasn't until Daniel was gone that this reality hit, so all I could feel was emptiness and betrayal.

But why?

As I looked and longed for answers, I wasn't confident that I would find any. The anger I had toward God and the confusion I had about healing made me temporarily reject God's Word as a source of answers. So then I was in a bad way but wasn't willing to look beyond myself for relief. I was stuck and felt empty.

People would try to help me by making comments like, "I could never have as much faith as you." At the time, I felt like they were complimenting me for my faith, not God for His work in me. I felt as though they were saying that they were impressed that I hadn't rejected my God for allowing this to happen, but if it were them, they'd be throwing God under the bus. Those thoughts were totally wrong, but at the time, I couldn't think any differently. The comments made by others were sincere and meant to console, but I wanted to use them as a weapon against God. I was mad that God took my son, so I would use anything said by anyone to prove that I was right and God was wrong.

I had a hard time connecting with comments about my strength of faith because of what I knew of my faith at that time too. I couldn't take God at His Word. I needed to know, not just read, that Daniel was in a better place, that God loved him, and that He was caring for him. I questioned why his life was cut short, why all the blessings of this life were withheld from him. I questioned the purpose, what was gained by Daniel's early departure from this life. These were all questions—or more accurately doubts—that didn't seem to represent someone with strong faith.

I was told that my anger and questions were all a part of the grieving process, but to me, that was an empty statement, because what it implied was that the questions I had would all go away once the grieving was over. Where was the good in that? I didn't want to just get over my loss; I had those questions because I either didn't have the appropriate understanding of God's Word or because I lacked faith. I knew that my anger was inappropriate, but I also knew that my questions would ultimately lead to growth, even though I resisted it.

Job started out thinking his relationship with God was a mature relationship, built on years of service, interaction, and love. Yet after God challenged his thinking, he realized that he had no right to question God's judgments because God's perspective is beyond comparison. Job realized that he really didn't know God that well prior to his trial and after was able to see God as He is. Job didn't just get over the grieving; his trial led to a much deeper connection with God.

The same is true in my walk with God. I talk about growing in faith, yet I resist the trials in life that will draw me closer to God and increase my faith. Then I become angry and bitter and feel abandoned by the one I want to draw closer to, blaming Him for my hurt and loss. Faith is not an event, or destination, or possession. Faith is a journey, the outcome of which is not to have more faith but to know the Father intimately, to yield to Him and trust Him for every need.

God knew I was angry. He knew that the source of my anger was my desire to control the situation, and He knew that this was because my worldview was too small. I really wasn't as at peace with death as I had once thought I was. God gave me time to move forward, but it became clear to me that He would not allow me to stay angry. He brought wonderful people into my life to prop me up. He surrounded me with love and drew me back to His Word for answers—answers to all the questions that were weighing me down.

Faith lives and grows as God draws us closer to Him. Throughout my life, God put the desire in me to know Him more intimately. I asked for it, but just like James and John, I really didn't know what I was asking for. They wanted to have positions that demonstrated their closeness and intimacy with Jesus but didn't realize that having that relationship with Him would require refining and trials that would draw them into that intimacy with Him (Matt 20:21–23). For me, the trial was to let go of control over my son and place him in God's hands, trusting that whatever the outcome was, Daniel would be okay because God loves him. I would never go there on my own, but God didn't leave me hanging. He took me there. He drew me to Himself by putting the desire in me to have that closeness with Him. Then He put this trial in my path to draw me to Him, but He also provided me with the strength to endure the trial.

Our Shepherd's Voice

As I considered people I would see in the waiting rooms of cancer centers, it occurred to me that the rooms were filled with people longing for healing. There was no laughing, no light conversation, and no joy. They were sick, scared, and longing for hope. There were so many of them. People come in droves to these medical centers where doctors do their best with the technology they have to heal them. As I looked into many of their eyes, they looked empty of hope and tired.

It brought me back to how I felt when I got the news of Daniel's sicknesses. The fog was thick, making it difficult for me to engage in anything meaningful. However, I didn't stay there long because I had hope—a hope that came from my relationship with God and the foundation I had in His Word. I had a friendship with God that allowed me to take all my cares and concerns for Daniel to Him, and I had many intimate conversations with Him that brought me a peace. I longed for all those people I saw in the hospitals to have that same relationship with God.

I once heard a story of a man who was in an upper floor of a high-rise building when a fire broke out in the floors below. Forgive me if you've heard this story and I don't get all the details right. I remember just enough of it to make my point. Everyone was able to get out of the building except that man. For some reason, he froze at the sign of danger and couldn't bring himself to leave.

The fire department soon came and set up to rescue him through a window. As they called to him, he was able to inch himself over to the window, from which the firefighters continually encouraged him to jump, telling him he would be okay. The problem was that the man couldn't see below because of the smoke and flames, so he couldn't bring himself to trust what the men were telling him and remained frozen at the window.

After some time of trying unsuccessfully to convince the man to jump, the firefighters were able to connect with the man's father. They gave him the microphone, and he then called up to his son. "Everything will be fine," he told him. "Just jump." The man recognized his dad's voice and knew that he could trust his dad, so that gave him the courage to leap from the window to safety.

That's how it is with healing, isn't it? We can be told to trust God, to let go of our fears and believe that He will heal us, but if we don't know His voice—if we don't know Him or if we don't know what He promises us about healing—then they are just empty words spoken by a stranger we aren't sure we can trust.

Is it possible for us to truly hear God's voice? There are so many voices inside our heads, some good, some bad, and some really bad. Can we say that the good thoughts are always God's and leave it at that? If so, then having ice cream every meal is a gift from God. Now that's a nice thought! But seriously, if we need a better compass to lead us to a connection with God's voice, where do we find it? How is it then that we know when God is speaking to us? How do we discern God's voice amongst all the noise inside our heads?

God does provide signs and speak directly to us at times, but those times are rare, and we can never plan or dictate when that will happen. In most cases, God speaks to our spirits. Without getting too far into the weeds regarding spiritual matters, let's look at what this means. Paul gives us a summary of how this works that will launch us into this discussion:

> We speak the wisdom of God in a mystery, the hidden wisdom which God ordained before the ages for our glory. (1 Cor 2:7)

> God has revealed them to us through His Spirit. For the Spirit searches all things, yes, the deep things of God. For what man knows the things of a man except the spirit of the man which is in him? Even so no one knows the things of God except the Spirit of God. Now we have received, not the spirit of the world, but the Spirit who is from God, that we might know the things that have been freely given to us by God. These things we also speak, not in words which man's wisdom teaches but which the Holy Spirit teaches, comparing spiritual things with spiritual. (1 Cor 2:10–13)

We all have a human spirit. We typically refer to it as the voice inside our head or our conscience. All the good and bad things we learn and experience in our lives are captured by our conscious or subconscious memory. Our spirit connects with our mind, accessing those memories, creating our thoughts.

Our spirit also connects us with the spiritual world around us. This allows our adversary to broadcast lies and negative ideas to us or use the destructive things we've learned and experienced against us. He wants our minds filled with only negative thoughts.

Then there is God's Spirit, which is made available to us. When we receive God's Spirit, He lives within us (Jn 14:16–17). The Spirit reveals the hidden mystery of God's wisdom to us, guides us into all truth (Jn 16:13), and teaches us and reminds us of all the things Jesus said (Jn 14:26). He speaks to us through that voice in our head. We know it's His voice as we read His Word and find alignment between what we are thinking and what His Word tells us. Discerning God's voice becomes easier and easier for us as we spend more and more time with Him through study, meditation, and prayer. It's not that we are obligated to do these things to have God's approval. Rather, God puts the desire in our hearts for intimacy with Him, so we seek Him out using these methods.

When the adversary attacks us by implanting negative thoughts in our heads, God's Spirit defends us using the scriptures (Eph 6:17). You can see where the battle lines are drawn. They're drawn inside your head. Your battle is a spiritual battle, the results of which you should never fear. Paul's encouragement is that the battle belongs to us:

> Yet in all these things we are more than conquerors through Him who loved us. For I am persuaded that neither death nor life, nor angels nor principalities nor powers, nor things present nor things to come, nor height nor depth, nor any other created thing, shall be able to separate us from the love of God which is in Christ Jesus our Lord. (Rom 8:37–39)

There, I just outlined the "mechanics" of what's going on inside your head. However, discerning God's voice isn't an event that just happens. As I've said before, our walk with God is a journey, not a destination. God will speak to you before you know Him. He will put a thought in your head that compels you to follow what you're being told even though you may not fully understand it. It may take a while before you realize that the message sent to you was from God, but then He will place the desire in you for more intimacy, so you will seek Him. And as you learn more and more of His ways, His voice will become easier and easier to discern.

The problem that will continually plague you is finding time for God. The busyness of life will continually pull you away from Him, and even when you do find time, your mind will be distracted. Even today as I spend one-on-one time with God, I struggle to keep myself in the moment. I am able to keep my mind focused on spiritual matters for only so long before a negative thought interrupts me. Sometimes it feels like minutes have gone by before I realize that my thoughts were carried away from God. Once that happens, it's always hard to find that moment again.

Don't let any of that deter you, though. Every moment you find to spend time with God is a moment that will bless you. As your relationship with God grows, your desire will be for more of your thoughts to be on Him and less of them to be in destructive places, and with this shift, there will be less of those negative experiences for your adversary to draw from. You will be able to identify negative thoughts sooner and ask God to replace those thoughts with proper thoughts. And when that happens—voila! You are discerning God's voice and allowing Him to lead your life.

Yet we do stumble. You will stumble. Remember, though: journey, not destination. You will be faced with challenges for which you want God's direction but find that the connection you have with Him doesn't seem to provide you with the answers you so desperately need. That happened to me. I clearly heard God's voice as He healed Daniel of the cancer yet felt lost and alone as I struggled through Daniel's last weeks. The problem for me, I now see, wasn't that God stopped being with me and communicating with me. The problem was that God wasn't providing me with the outcome I so desperately desired. God never left my side. He never stopped communicating with me, but it took a long time for me to recognize that.

My hope for you is that you have God to lean on during your trial. It doesn't matter where you are in your walk with God because God will meet you there. Talk to Him and listen to what He has for you and your loved one.

Giving up Control / The Rest That God Gives

The Bible says that when we are able to trust God, evidenced by the surrender of our fears into His hands, we find rest. Understanding God's rest is another one of those topics with which you can get so far out into the weeds that you lose the simplicity of God's intention. God wants intimacy with us. He wants us to lay all our burdens on Him. Jesus says:

> "Come to Me, all you who labor and are heavy laden, and I will give you rest. Take My yoke upon you and learn from Me, for I am gentle and lowly in heart, and you will find rest for your souls. For My yoke is easy and My burden is light." (Matt 11:28–30)

God wants us to give up all the issues that are weighing us down or causing us to worry. He wants us to trust Him and allow Him to teach us. He will carry our burdens for us.

When someone asks you to trust them, what's the first thing that comes to your mind? It's skepticism, isn't it? You asking me to trust you automatically puts me in a defensive mode with you. Why should I trust you? You certainly won't trust someone you don't know, especially if they're encouraging you to.

Our walk with God is no different. We can be encouraged to trust God until we're blue in the face, but it won't mean anything to us unless we know God. God doesn't want us to blindly trust Him either. Remember, He wants intimacy with us. Trusting Him is a by-product of that intimacy.

Resting in God is the most intimate response to God's love for you. It means trusting Him with the most cherished possessions you have. For me, it means allowing Him to watch over my family and trusting that whatever happens in their lives is for their ultimate good. That's easy to say. Who wouldn't want to have all the things that we worry and stress about removed, especially the important things like the welfare of family members? Prior to Daniel's sickness, I would pray every morning that God would protect my family, prosper them, and draw them closer to Him. Yet to trust God with the healing of Daniel was one of the most difficult things for me to do. I would continually find myself reacting to issues that came up by taking charge. It didn't matter what the issue was; when we were faced with a new challenge, my first response was to act on it.

Whether we want to admit it or not, our nature demands that we control our environment. You don't need to look very far to see evidence of this. The story of Adam and Eve is a perfect example of how, left to ourselves, we will always do things our way and reject what God teaches us. The freedom to speak and think as we want is a basic human desire. Just look at how highly freedom of speech is regarded. And consider toddlers. Somewhere between learning to talk and preschool, the "little monsters" learn that Mom and Dad's requests aren't in their best interest and so begin to go a different way—their way. No matter how hard the parent tries to keep the word *no* out of their vocabulary, it always seems to be one of those key words they learn.

We talk affectionately about how God will carry us through the trials of life. As I look back on our journey, I realize that God had to pick me up and carry me into the trial as well. I fought. I fought hard to maintain control. I couldn't just rest in God. As soon as an issue came up, I needed to find a solution. I would pray, but then I would jump into action. It wasn't as though I was consciously doing that. Yet before I could realize what was going on, I was already knee-deep in finding a solution and unraveling emotionally.

On one occasion, we were working through a somewhat routine activity that caused me to have a meltdown. Daniel had completed the first three months of treatment in his clinical trial and was scheduled for a bone marrow biopsy that we all knew would show that he was cured from the cancer. He had the biopsy and then met with the doctor. As it ended up, the biopsy results would not be known for a week, but he still had one lymph node that was swollen and was complaining about soreness. Now, the biopsy results would eventually come back confirming that Daniel's body was clear of the disease, but we didn't know that at the time. So, although Daniel's remaining symptoms were not really a concern for the doctor, I found myself searching for information on what could possibly be happening, which led to all kinds of what ifs. I was trying to process why the healing hadn't come and what the relationship between the cancer, swollen lymph nodes, and soreness meant. I was determined to find the answer. Consequently, in a very short period of time, I went from anticipation and hope for complete healing to despair. Let me tell you, that's a scary place to be! How easy it was for me to turn my focus from God to trusting in myself and taking matters into my own hands.

I didn't like living there. Stepping outside that place of rest with God is unsettling, uncomfortable, and … well … scary. The minute I got there, I realized that this was a place I no longer wanted to be. Yet why did I find it so easy to look away from God? Why was it that I still wanted to take on troubles by myself when I knew that it would lead to separation from God, making a mess of my situation, or despairing without hope? But that's the human condition, isn't it?

That's one of the things the garden of Eden represents for us. Our nature is to reject God's nurturing and guidance and go it alone. We want to decide for ourselves what is right and what is wrong. We want control of our lives and will fight desperately to maintain that control. So then, when we talk about our walk with God, what we're really talking about is learning to live every breath of our lives connected to God, trusting in Him, and looking to Him for all our needs—simply stated, resting in God.

In truly trusting God, I had to be okay with whatever direction God chose for Daniel, yet emotionally I struggled to deal with the potential loss of him. My heart's desire was for Daniel to know God as well as experience all the good in life that God had for him, so I was torn and lacking the trust to just let go. Even now, I am prone to keep holding on to control over my life, my family's well-being, my issues, and my problems instead of just holding on to my Father and resting in the fact that He knows what's best for me, wants what's best for me, and will utilize His ultimate power to carry out what's best for me.

David cried out to God to lead him back when his heart was overwhelmed (Psalm 61:2). But resting in God isn't just turning to Him in times of trouble; it's staying in His presence always, in good times and in bad. It's knowing that there's no better place to be and that no matter what comes our way, He's got our back.

There are others who have gone before us and experienced similar struggles. Fortunately, we have a record of their struggles to learn from. Consider Abraham, known to Israel as the father of the faith. He believed and trusted in God, so God considered him to be righteous. Yet even Abraham faltered when God promised that his descendants would be as numerous as the stars in the sky. He initially believed, but as the years passed and he still wasn't blessed with a son, he began to doubt. How could he and Sarah have a child since she was way beyond her childbearing years? So he took matters into his own hands and had a child with one of Sarah's handmaids. Abraham took his eyes off God. He considered his circumstances and came to the conclusion that what he desired was physically impossible. Sounds familiar, doesn't it?

I'm not into cookie-cutter methods for achieving a closer relationship with God. God broke me of that trap a long time ago. As I've mentioned before, like with so much of our walk with God, trusting in Him is definitely a journey and not a destination. It takes practice, so you have to start taking more and more of your concerns to Him. You also need to be aware of His presence with you and His response to your concerns. Even then, as we've seen, there will come times when God asks you to do things that challenge your trust.

Always remember, though, that God is for you like no one else.

Spiritual Warfare

The entertainment world has done a wonderful job of glamorizing our spiritual adversary while at the same time causing us to feel unsophisticated if we believe in a spiritual world or the notion of an adversary. That doesn't make their characterization truth, however. We have a very real spiritual adversary who wants to bring us down and turn us from God. His methods are subtle yet effective. He communicates thoughts to us that make us doubt and lose hope. Paul warns us that our adversary has power over the airwaves (Eph 2:2). He is able to broadcast thoughts to us that will become a part of our consciousness if we let them. This reality was driven home for me in a profound way during Daniel's sickness.

A spiritual battle was going on inside of me. It happened in the form of negative thoughts continually yet subtly being placed in my mind. Thoughts of whether God was healing or would heal Daniel kept bombarding me. They would come when my eyes had been taken off God, or they would just randomly show up. Suddenly, they would be there. Sometimes I was able to recognize the nature of the thoughts immediately and remove or replace them, but other times I would get caught up in them before recognizing them for what they were: an attack from my adversary.

It's like the story of the time Jesus and His followers were in a boat crossing a lake when a windstorm came up (Matt 8:24–26). The disciples' immediate reaction was to panic and call for Jesus to save them, and without hesitation, Jesus calmed the winds for them. Now, His followers were continuously present with Him. They witnessed all of His miracles, so they had no need to panic, yet their physical circumstances overcame their knowledge. And so it was with me. I was able to fight off attacks when I stayed connected to God, but as soon as I drifted, the attacks were there.

Over and over again, I would run into people or circumstances that would try to bring me down and turn my eyes away from God. Many times, the attacks were unintentional or even thought to be uplifting or helpful. Some people would want to confirm that I wasn't just relying on faith for Daniel's healing, while others would give me very specific instructions on how to pray for healing and what my attitude needed to be toward healing. Doctors would totally ignore God and give me very clinical responses to what they could provide for Daniel and what the ultimate outcome would be.

Doctor visits and test results were continually a spiritual battle for me because even though I was committed to waiting on God's timing for the healing to come, I was always hopeful that each visit would be the one when the results would be positive or the doctors would give me uplifting news.

Through it all, though, there was God and His Word and His promises keeping me strong. He was my foundation. When I interpreted scripture to my advantage, God brought me back to a right understanding. When my adversary broadcasted negative thoughts, God reminded me of His promises for healing. And when people brought me down with their words, God lifted me up with His Word.

Our adversary wants us to stay grieving and drive us to self-pity. He does this by continually trying to break us down and turn us from God. In my situation, he kept putting the memories of Daniel's last days and the pain and suffering he went through in my mind. He also caused me to question why so much had happened to such a young man with his whole life in front of him. These kinds of thoughts are destructive. They keep us buried in the past and then turn and harden us against God.

God doesn't block these thoughts from us, although I believe He only allows our adversary to attack us in ways He's prepared us for. Instead, He gives us true thoughts to replace the negative, ugly ones. When I am hit with thoughts of Daniel's death and his life being over, God reminds me that Daniel is alive, Daniel is with Him, and Daniel will be resurrected with an eternal body in the near future. When my adversary attacks me with thoughts of the pain and suffering he went through, God reminds me that he no longer suffers and the sting of death is gone. When my adversary attacks me by raising the question of God's purpose for taking Daniel at such a young age and overwhelming me with memories of my loss, God reminds me of His amazing love for Daniel, how He wants so much more for Daniel than I could ever imagine, how He cherishes the day Daniel returned to Him, and how we will be reunited with him, to be brothers and sisters with Daniel in God's kingdom forevermore. That's how God is carrying me through these difficult times.

We all need to acknowledge that we have a spiritual adversary and be aware of his methods. Our adversary wants to destroy you. He wants you to ask why. He wants you to be confused. He wants you to grieve and stay in a place of being alone and disconnected from God. He will attack you with painful realities, peer pressure, and intellectual arguments based on physical circumstances. He will twist the truth just enough to make it a cleverly disguised lie. He is real, and he wants to keep separation between you and your loving Father.

But God is there. God is for you, so nothing and no one can stand against you. God is there to protect you. He will give you whatever you need to move forward in whatever your circumstances are. You just need to ask.

Conclusion

The book of Hebrews tells us that faith is the realization of things hoped for and the confidence of things not seen (Heb 11:1). Prior to Daniel's passing away, I never deeply considered this verse. I thought my faith was sufficient, like a prized possession I had. However, the realization that this life is temporary and my only hope for Daniel is in his resurrection exposed my lack of faith. I wanted to believe and could intellectually make that connection, yet I found myself frustrated by the fact that I truly didn't know what lay beyond this life. That caused me to doubt God's care and provision for Daniel.

I really struggled with the idea that God could somehow be glorified through suffering or death. I knew that personally I draw much closer to Him when I'm in conflict or suffering. (The good times are a wonderful gift from God, but I typically get caught up in living life when things are good, so my contact and connection with Him tend to be more superficial.) However, I didn't see how others could view what happened to Daniel as anything but tragic. As time has passed, I've come to realize that this line of thinking was all a part of me desperately trying to control the situation and not surrendering Daniel's life, his entire life, to God.

When Daniel passed away, I was mad at God because He didn't do what I wanted Him to do. I created a wall between me and God. Yet my spirit was troubled and couldn't find comfort because I was reluctant to go to the one source that was able to provide me with that comfort. I kept trying to find reasons to stay angry with God. I would tell myself that going to God's Word for comfort wasn't enough because they were just words, and words could not bring me comfort. I needed to know, not just read, that Daniel was okay. I would then demand that God provide me with a vision of the future.

God patiently waited on me, all the while prompting me to know that my questions could only be answered by Him. The question of what lies beyond this life is spiritual in nature, so where else could I turn for answers but to God?

God drew me into Him and His Word, and there He provided answers to all my questions. Going back into His Word illuminated for me the love He has for us, His children, and the amazing future that awaits us. This understanding has brought me peace and comfort and provided me with a way to move forward in spite of the loss.

As I look back on my time here on this earth, I see that my journey of faith has taken me in many directions. There have been pleasant travels when I have been able to recognize the wonderful blessings God has for me in life and difficult times when the storms of life have forced me to trust God in ways I wasn't initially able to or for that matter wanting to.

What God has done for me is carry me through each day, each difficult moment, each flashback, and each conversation in which I have been asked how I'm doing. It's not that my beliefs are now so strong that I just get it and everything's okay. I don't think God works that way. He wants me to experience the loss and grieve for my son and recognize that this place we're in today is not perfect and not the outcome He has envisioned for us. He wants me to question Him and seek answers because that brings me into intimacy with Him.

God has propped me up and carried me through this trial in my life. I know that any strength to breathe or courage to face the day has come from Him, and I am so thankful for that. I may have struggled to see my faith in all of this, but I now realize that I could never have faced this trial on my own. It is God and only God who is carrying me through.

I know that my faith is much stronger today than it was prior to

Daniel's sicknesses. But I also know that I have a long way to go, and God is not done with me yet. In some ways, that causes me to be a little unsettled, but I know that God loves me like no other, so I will rest in that, knowing that whatever happens, He is there for me.

When you're faced with a significant trial, it will be difficult. Growth is painful. You will be required to submit to God's direction, yet you won't want to. You will try to maintain control of events as they unfold before you. You will falter and fall. You will face frustration or even lash out in anger toward God as I did. The walls you construct between you and God will be different from mine, but there will be walls that you create.

If you're feeling lost, know that God is there for you. There is nothing you can say or do to drive God away. He will prompt you to move forward. He will reveal His love to you. However, it's up to you to react. Will you allow your situation to keep you in a constant state of mourning or destroy you? Or will you allow God to lead you to peace? As you read on, my prayer for you is that your perspective on this life will be changed as God reveals His love for us and the amazing destiny He has in store for us.

chapter 6

God's Love

Throughout our fight for Daniel's health, we were faced many times with another adversary: the medical professionals responsible for his care. Unfortunately, there were several instances when the care that Daniel received was woefully inadequate, and a few of them are burned into my memory. The first came after we learned that Daniel's oncologist was leaving the hospital and Daniel's next visit would be with the hospital's top CLL specialist.

We didn't think much of it; the visit was considered nothing more than routine. We were hoping that the report would be positive, that Daniel's white blood cell count was reducing or staying consistent. Instead, what we got was bad news, and from a doctor who really didn't care about Daniel. It was painfully obvious that the doctor was more concerned with his investments than building his patients up or showing any kind of concern for them. He ridiculed Daniel for working for a business that was struggling to stay open, smugly pronouncing that the company's stock was only worth a dollar. He then told Daniel that his white blood cell count was rising at a pretty good clip and that he would need to start treatment fairly soon. When Gretchen responded that we'd pray and hope for the best, the doctor came back with, "That's not going to happen."

We were all trying to stay upbeat and positive, but needless to say, the visit got everyone pretty down. For the next several days, we were back in that cycle of discouragement, searching for answers, prayer, feeling peace for the moment, and then discouragement again.

The next situation occurred when Daniel had been diagnosed with congestive heart failure and went back to the emergency room because of the pain in his abdomen and groin. At that point, the doctors told us he also had an inguinal hernia. That diagnosis was hard enough for us to wrap our minds around, but when Daniel started vomiting the next week, we were concerned that might mean the hernia was now strangulated. We took Daniel back to the emergency room for a third time, but the doctors were content just sending him home again. That, of course, wasn't satisfactory to us. We pressed them to figure out what was going on, and finally they did a CT scan and told us that Daniel didn't have a hernia after all. The pain that he was having was because his abdomen was full of fluid and he was getting fluid in his lungs.

We asked the doctor if he had communicated this to Daniel's cardiologist, and he told us he hadn't because he had already discussed Daniel's condition with him earlier in the day. The cardiologist told the emergency room doctor he never believed that Daniel had a hernia in the first place and was in a "wait and see" mode with his condition, so he wasn't planning to do anything more for him. The emergency room doctor then told us they could hold Daniel overnight to do more tests on his gallbladder because the CT scan showed swelling there.

At this point, the reality of what was happening was clear to us. Daniel had congestive heart failure, the medicines he was given weren't working, his abdomen was filling with fluids, his organs were swelling—it seemed as though Daniel was going into cardiogenic shock while the doctors wanted to "wait and see" what was going to happen. They were willing to pacify us, though, by admitting Daniel and doing further tests on his gallbladder.

We told the hospital we would not have Daniel admitted and demanded that he be sent to another hospital. The hospital resisted our request, telling us that there wasn't anything any other hospital could provide for Daniel that they couldn't provide there, but we were adamant. Needless to say, it took forever to get the hospital motivated to make the move, to contact and get approval from the receiving hospital and organize transportation. Of course, though, they had us pay for the ambulance up front before they would do anything.

The final situation occurred as we tried desperately to get Daniel transported to Cedars-Sinai Hospital to have a heart transplant. Without going into too much detail, let's just say that the doctors resisted us every step of the way. I will never fully understand why they acted the way they did toward us, but I think the bottom line is that we were forcing them to do something they didn't want to do. They were not happy with the fact that they were being forced to support transporting Daniel to another hospital that had more expertise than they did.

The anger and downright hatred they had toward us weren't initially evident. We were in such a fog and were focused on trying to save our son's life, so their attitudes never even crossed our minds. They did, however, become so hurtfully obvious to us as the doctors brought us into the meeting room to tell us the tragic news about Daniel. One of the doctors was smiling as we walked by. At the time, only a few of us noticed, but that gave us the momentary thought that they must be about to tell us good news.

As the head neurologist explained what had happened to Daniel, everyone broke down except me. I looked at each doctor and then looked off into space, waiting for a miracle to happen. My thought was interrupted when the doctor who had been smiling as we walked in spoke. She looked directly at me and emphatically stated, "So he won't be going to Cedars-Sinai."

From that point on, I started to recognize an angry tone in many of the staff as we worked through Daniel's last hours. At the time, their hatred meant nothing to me. I had just lost my beloved son. However, in the weeks and months after, I found those events continually entering my mind, causing me to question, why?

It's hard to understand cruelty directed at us by people who didn't even know us. I thought they were there to help us. I thought helping others was their job. Why would they treat us with such indifference? Why would they be so cruel? Was fighting for our son's life an unreasonable request? I was confused. I thought the doctors would surely understand that a parent would never give up on saving their child if there was even one sliver of hope. Even if the doctors don't have anyone they cherish in their lives, isn't that common sense? Why are they in the medical profession if they don't care about people? Is professional or academic pride that strong that it overtakes any sense of compassion toward patients?

Oddly enough, my anger never manifested itself toward the doctors. They were only ever instruments used by God to bring care to Daniel. I'd always known that if any healing was going to occur, it would come from God, so then I was mad at God. I struggled to see how God could love me yet allow us to face these attitudes and cruelties on top of dealing with Daniel's sicknesses.

I was brought up in a Christian home, so I've known of God's love for me from an early age. I've also experienced God's care for me. In countless situations, I've needed help, clarity, direction, or answers, and every time, I've taken those situations to Him. He's provided for my needs, so I've always known that He's there watching over me, that He loves me.

I can look back and see how God was working with me from a young age. As a kid, I would look at the Bible displayed in our living room, and the thought would come to me that God's truth was somewhere hidden within its pages. I would try to read it but wasn't ready or willing to commit my life to a relationship with God.

As a young adult, I did many, many stupid and dangerous things I'm not proud of. Looking back, I can see how God protected me from my stupidity and directed me, yet I still refused to turn to Him. Finally, in college, I got to a point where I had totally messed up everything. I wasn't working. I had a huge amount of student loan debt. I was kicked out of school for failing every class. And I was partying heavily. It was at that point that I broke down and asked God to forgive me and pleaded with Him to take over my life because I couldn't continue on that way.

In a quiet, calm voice, God told me to start working (I know, earth-shattering, right?). The next morning, I found a job opening in the paper. I was interviewed that day and started working the next. That was the changing point in my life. Thankfully, God never gave up on me. I wasn't the one who brought about the changes in my life; it was God and God alone!

Yet as I mentioned before, in Daniel's last days, as his condition continually deteriorated, it seemed as though God had abandoned us. This left me feeling like I couldn't trust God anymore and caused me to question what God's love really is. How can I experience God's love when

I can't see Him? If God truly loved me, would He abandon me in my time of most need? It also made me consider that all those scriptures showing and defining God's love for us were merely words. What good are words when your experiences tell a different story?

I was unraveling emotionally, which caused me to think irrational thoughts. All the years I walked with God should have prepared me for what stood before me, yet I was now in a place where I couldn't describe God's love for me beyond the written words of the Bible.

I know that this is where you're at. All of your life experiences have brought you to this point. You should be able to handle whatever it is that God has placed before you, but now that you're here, you feel so completely unequipped to handle it. You don't know how to face the next step. You want and need something tangible. You want healing. You want a sign. You need to know that everything will be okay. You need to feel God's presence, but He seems more distant than ever.

You're not alone. Jesus felt what you are feeling. His prayer to the Father as He anticipated what was coming (although He would do whatever the Father willed) was that He would take His trial away from Him: "O My Father, if this cup cannot pass away from Me unless I drink it, Your will be done" (Matt 26:42). He endured ridicule, beatings, and betrayal from His own people. He was innocent, yet He endured scourging and the shame of dying on a tree outside the gates of the city. And finally, as He reached the end of His suffering, He cried out, "My God, My God, why have You forsaken Me?" (Matt 27:46). He temporarily felt the absence of God there with Him in His time of most need.

Jesus experienced everything that you and I have experienced and more. He knows your suffering. He knows your need, and He is there with you. He will never leave you or your loved ones' side. You will experience loss. You will grieve. You will question God and feel anger toward Him. But regardless of how you react, He will not leave you.

God's Love Manifested in Those around You

When you face trials of the most devastating kind, God knows that head knowledge is not enough, so He will surround you with the love of others

He has prepared for you to physically demonstrate his love. Through those people, God will provide you with everything you need to move forward.

In the days following Daniel's departure, I retreated back to God's Word. I desperately needed to know that he was okay, so I searched the scriptures to find passages that talked of God's love for us. My thought was that if I could read what God told me about His love for us, somehow I would find peace and comfort, somehow my questions would all go away. As I made my way through the scriptures, there was a calmness that came from just being in God's Word, but I still felt empty. They were still just words. I needed something more tangible than words.

I wanted to believe what I was reading, but at the time I couldn't see beyond the fog. Granted, God was there with me helping me through the countless details of each day; I knew that. Both Gretchen and I were propped up in ways we never would have been on our own. Yet when I needed God the most, in a life-and-death situation, He was silent. So I questioned how I truly knew what God's love for Daniel (and all of us) was.

This led me to turn to the evidence in my life. I considered my relationship with my sons. Did I ever make a decision that I knew my sons wouldn't like because they were too young to understand my reasoning but that I went forward with anyway without explaining myself to them?

The answer, of course, was yes, several times.

Had there ever been times when the things my sons wanted seemed like the most important things in the world to them, but I knew that there were more important things to consider and that their perspective was very self-centered?

Yes.

Were they ever mad at me for denying their requests?

Yes.

Would I give them some space to work through their anger with me before talking to them again?

Sometimes too much space.

And would I have Gretchen talk to them to let them know they were still loved?

Yes again.

I always wanted the boys to know I loved them. Sometimes I was quick to get back with them and ensure that our relationship was intact, but most often it would be Gretchen mending things. Gretchen was always there to fill the void.

When I reached that consideration, I realized what God was doing. I looked around and saw acquaintances, close friends, and family members carrying all our burdens and providing for all our physical and emotional needs. How had I missed it before? All those wonderful people who surrounded us with love were sent by God to us. While I was crying out to God to show Himself to me and comfort me, God kept sending angels to us. He has and is sending angels to you also.

You see, God is love (1 Jn 4:8), so everything He creates is an expression of that love. When God created humankind, He extended His love to us with the gift of family—being His family and having our own families. He also created us with the capacity to love and the desire to experience love. Any act of love we experience or observe in others is from God and is a reflection of God's character and His love for us. Let me say that again. *Any act of love* we experience or observe in others is from God and is a reflection of God's character and His love for us.

We don't need to see God in person or hear a voice thunder, "I love you," or have Him touch us when we experience an expression of love to know His love. We experience His love in every loving interaction we have with anyone. It doesn't matter what our nationality or religion or social status is. After all, we're all family. We're all God's children and therefore brothers and sisters. Love is not a character trait inherent in humanity apart from God. We don't just love because it's our nature. We love because God is love and He created us in His image; He created us in love to love.

This was one of the central messages that Jesus brought to us. Everything He did, He did out of love for us. His interactions and teachings were all designed to break us free from religion and false worship and bring us into a correct, loving relationship with our Father and each other. When asked which of God's commandments was the greatest, Jesus replied that the first and great commandment was to love God with all our heart, soul, and mind. He then went on to add that the second greatest command was to love our neighbors as ourselves (Matt 22:34–40; Mk 12:28–31). There are no other commandments greater than these. The apostle John helped connect these two commandments for us by telling us that we cannot love

God if we don't love one another. If we don't love someone we can see, how can we love God, whom we cannot see (1 Jn 4:20)?

This was the point I was missing and why I wasn't recognizing God's love in my time of need. I wanted acknowledgment from God that He was there. I wanted a feeling of warmth when no one else was around that was an expression of God's love. God didn't give me what I wanted, but He did give me what I needed. He surrounded me with people who gave of themselves and had a love for Him that was reflected in everything they did. If I had been watching, I would have understood God's love for me through the love showered upon me by the people God sent me.

Take a moment to reflect back on all the wonderful people God has brought to you. Some have always been there for you; they're your anchors. And there are likely others who have stepped up their game as this difficulty has come upon you or people you would have never expected to be there for you who are right there by your side. They were all prepared for you and sent to you by God.

How can I thank all the wonderful people who gathered around us, and propped us up, and comforted us, and cried with us, and shared good memories with us? Some just took over. They knew what needed to be done and started doing it. They were there with us from the very beginning of Daniel's sicknesses. On one occasion, I had just gotten some bad news, but I was at work, so I felt like there was nowhere for me to go to work through and process what I'd been told. I remember walking through the cafeteria and spotting a cherished friend. He must have recognized that something was wrong, so he pulled me aside right there in the cafeteria and prayed with me. That same person became someone who God prepared for me to lean on countless times for prayer. Who is that person in your life?

Another good friend who was close to Daniel wanted to come to the hospital and visit with him. He drove all the way to the hospital only to be turned away because Daniel had just received some bad news and was waiting to be told what the next steps, if any, would be. Even though he couldn't see Daniel, he came to me at a time when I was broken and needed someone to come alongside me. As soon as I started talking to him, I broke down. It wasn't something I had planned on doing; it just happened. As soon as I saw him, the reality of what was happening all came to the surface and overwhelmed me. We prayed together, and then I went back to Daniel's side while this friend stayed in the waiting room for a while to pray for us. You can't plan how these events will unfold. They are ordained by God to come to you at the times you most need them.

Then there was a group from work that actively supported people in need of healing or prayer. They created a beautiful collage using one thousand origami cranes. These wonderful ladies made every one of those cranes by hand with Daniel in their hearts. When it was presented to him, he was speechless and shed a few tears of gratitude. We are only one of many families those ladies have supported with their wonderful act of love.

Some people came and sat with us, providing much-needed perspective or just listening while we talked. They would sit with us for hours, allowing us to process the painful journey we had been on. Even though it would hurt to relive the events that had unfolded, there was healing there as we were able to express our inner thoughts. One conversation in particular touched me. A good friend walked us through a near-death experience he had when he was a young man. What really stayed with me was his description of the overwhelming sense of belonging and peace he experienced at the place where he went to while he was unconscious. At the time, I needed the assurance that Daniel was okay and being cared for, so I cherished those words expressed to me that day. God clearly sent him to me with that message.

Some provided meals for us whenever there was a situation that caused us to be in hospitals for extended periods of time. Some would sneak into our house and do all the cleaning for us. We were so appreciative to not have to cook or clean for at least two weeks after Daniel passed away. Some took care of our lawn for us. They would just show up with all their yard supplies to mow and care for our flowerbeds and then leave.

Some sent cards with thoughts and prayers attached, while others stood back because they were unsure, yet when I would see them, their concern for me was evident in their expressions and words. It's difficult to know how to act in times of sorrow. I was one of those people who stood back in the past, so I know that feeling and can recognize when someone is being sincere and their heart truly cries out to you in your sorrow, even if they don't stand out. However, I will tell you that as I move forward, I hope that I will have the courage to give anyone grieving a big, firm bear hug as soon as I see them. Individually, the hugs I received were thoughtful and genuine, and collectively, they brought healing.

I could go on listing the family members and friends who surrounded us and supported us forever. Sarah's friend set up a GoFundMe site, and Daniel's cousins made T-shirts that could be purchased to support Daniel's medical costs. One of Gretchen's dear friends started setting up a fundraiser to help with medical costs for a transplant. My cousin offered up her house to us in California once we arrived. My sister-in-law tried making connections with the insurance company to make sure someone stayed focused on Daniel's needs, and she was able to engage a family friend who had contacts with the insurance company. He was able to alert them of the situation, ensuring that there were no communication breaks and that Daniel's case would get immediate attention. Daniel's father-in-law made sure we had a medical transport ready in case the hospital dropped the ball. And armies of people were praying for Daniel's healing and that God would open whatever closed doors stood before us.

You have armies of people surrounding you that love you and will be with you every step of the way. Everything they do is being orchestrated by God. He is not distant in your time of need. He is right there, ensuring that every step you take has the appropriate support in place for you to move forward. He is also with your loved one, surrounding them with an unfailing love.

Jesus's Perfect Example of Love

Our culture today has a warped sense of what love really is. When we fall in love, all too often what we're really experiencing is lust or infatuation. We love our families but also love bunnies, chocolate, and sitcoms. We show more concern for animals and the environment than we show the homeless. Instead of loving others, we're bombarded with advertisements and broadcasts centered on loving ourselves.

Yet with all that, God's message of love is universally understood from generation to generation and across cultures. If we consider how we want to be treated and loved, we know and understand how God wants us to treat others. All the commandments pertaining to our relationship with others are summed up in loving our neighbors as ourselves (Gal 5:14; Jas 2:8).

Love does no harm to a neighbor; therefore, it fulfills all of God's desires for us (Rom 13:8–10). We all know what it's like to be down, or sad, or lonely, or heartbroken, or suffering, or grieving, so we need to reach out to others and treat them in a way that connects with how we ourselves want to be treated in those situations. By doing so, we are showing a sincere, genuine love to those in need—God's love.

When Jesus walked the earth, He provided us with an example of perfect love. He tells us that we are to love one another as He loved us. If we love each other in this way, all will know that we are His followers (Jn 13:34–35). And how did He love us? He died for us. "Greater love has no one than this, than to lay down one's life for his friends," He says (Jn 15:13). He became a man and gave up His life so that we could be one with God again (1 Jn 3:16–19). Now, we are to walk in His love as He loved us (Eph 5:2). We should have the same kind of sacrificial love for each other.

Our demonstration of love for others won't look exactly like Jesus's. We more than likely won't die in the stead of anyone else. But Jesus gave us so many other demonstrations of His kind of love to help us see what our lives could look like. On one occasion, a young lawyer, wanting to make himself right with God, asked Jesus who He considered his neighbor when He commanded, "Love your neighbor as yourself." Jesus replied by telling him the story of the Good Samaritan:

> "A certain man went down from Jerusalem to Jericho, and fell among thieves, who stripped him of his clothing, wounded him, and departed, leaving him half dead. Now by chance a certain priest came down that road. And when he saw him, he passed by on the other side. Likewise a Levite, when he arrived at the place, came and looked, and passed by on the other side. But a certain Samaritan, as he journeyed, came where he was. And when he saw him, he had compassion. So he went to him and bandaged his wounds, pouring on oil and wine; and he set him on his own animal, brought him to an inn, and took care of him. On the next day, when he departed, he took out two denarii, gave them to the innkeeper, and said to him,

'Take care of him; and whatever more you spend, when I come again, I will repay you.'" (Lk 10:30–35)

Our neighbor is everyone. There are no social, economic, national, or cultural exceptions. We are all God's children, so we are all each other's neighbors.

If someone asks you to go one mile with them, go two (Matt 5:41–42). Give to those who ask, and when you see someone's need, provide for it. When someone is hungry, give them food. When someone is thirsty, give them a drink. When someone is a stranger, take them in. When someone is in need of clothing, give them some. When someone is sick, visit them. And when someone is in prison, go to them. Love without hypocrisy. Be kind and affectionate. Honor others, giving preference to them above yourself. Rejoice with those who rejoice; weep with those who weep (Rom 12:9–21; Matt 25:35–40). And when someone loses their son, come alongside them and be the love of God to them.

I can honestly say that I fail in most if not all of these measures. My nature has always led me to be more self-absorbed, so in many cases, I'm not even aware of others in need, even when they're standing right in front of me. I've seen growth in myself as God has continued to soften my heart, but I know there is still much more I can and should do for others. I am truly grateful to God for having patience with my selfishness and blessing me by bringing so many of His angels to me. Just imagine what the world would be like if we all loved one another in these ways. I guess this gives us something to pray for and look forward to.

Again, all of God's expectations for us can be summed up by loving our neighbors as ourselves. When we are in need, we want people to come alongside us and help us, so we should be willing to do the same for others. We always want people to be accepting of us and to not offend us, so we should be willing to do the same for others.

With all the thoughtful acts of kindness my family experienced from all those who came to us in our time of need, what we were witnessing was a willingness on their part to serve us. Jesus, in a very profound way, taught us to have a heart of service. In the culture of His day, people wore sandals and walked on dirt roads, so their feet would become very dirty. It was therefore customary for the lowest person in the household to wash the feet of guests when they entered the home. But Jesus, our God and Creator of all things, washed the feet of each of His followers on the night before He gave His life for us. He told them to serve others as He was serving them (Jn 13:14–17).

If you've never taken part in a foot-washing ceremony, I suggest you do some day. Typically, you wash the feet of another person, and then they wash your feet. It's a very humbling experience that creates a bond of service and love between you and the other individual. When we serve others, we are doing the service for the Lord (1 Tim 6:2; Eph 6:7–8).

God illuminated His love for me by surrounding me with countless people who wanted nothing more than to be there for my family and me and provide any service to us that would lessen our pain. I truly witnessed God's love through all their selfless acts of kindness. As long as I live, I will carry the memory of each of these expressions of God's love with me.

My prayer for anyone grieving is that God would surround you too with armies of loving angels and that He would open your eyes to embrace these acts of kindness and compassion. For those of you who are not grieving firsthand but walking through grief with others, I pray that your heart's desire is toward serving your friend in need.

Adversaries

We are nothing without love. "Love suffers long and is kind; love does not envy; love does not parade itself, is not puffed up; does not behave rudely, does not seek its own, is not provoked, thinks no evil; does not rejoice in iniquity, but rejoices in the truth; bears all things, believes all things, hopes all things, endures all things." Everything else will eventually go away or fail, but love never fails. As followers of Jesus Christ, we need faith, hope, and love, "but the greatest of these is love" (1 Cor 13:2–7, 13).

It's easy for us to love those who love us; even evil people do that. But we are called to love also those who are our enemies, to give without expecting anything in return, to be kind to the unthankful and evil, and to be merciful just as God is merciful (Lk 6:32–36; Matt 5:43–47). This is a tall order. It's easy (or should I say easier) to love family, friends, and people whom we like or who like us. God wants more than that from us, though. We are to love those who hate us or hurt us. We cannot do this of our own ability. It takes God's Spirit living within us to bring about this transformation in our hearts. Stephen provides a good example for us of this kind of love for those who hurt us that transcends the evil. When He was being stoned by the Jews for following Jesus, He cried out to God to forgive the people stoning him. He then died (Act 7:57–60).

I've never considered that I had enemies in my life. I've had people I didn't connect with and stayed away from, but I can't say that there's been anyone I hated or who hated me (at least that I'm aware of). I tend to be very easygoing, and there are few things about which I have such a strong opinion or belief that it causes friction to the point of damaging a relationship.

However, I found that when it came to the care of my beloved son, I had very high expectations of the doctors involved and really struggled with some of the attitudes I encountered, especially at the end. I couldn't understand the callousness of some. I realized that not everyone would have the same sense of urgency that I did, but I thought we were all there for the same purpose—to save a life. I've had to let go of my anger toward some of the doctors and administrators who were over Daniel's care. I don't believe that I still harbor bad feelings for them, but I have a newfound appreciation for God's direction for me concerning my love for those who hurt me. If it was left to my capacity to forgive, there would be no forgiveness. Thankfully, God has given me a new heart. Moving forward, I know that this will continue to be a challenge for me and my family, so my prayer is that God will help us to always reflect His love toward others and forgive those whose actions hurt Daniel.

And as for my anger toward God, I know that God did not abandon my beloved son Daniel. God did not abandon His beloved child Daniel. Daniel is with our God of love now, in His presence. God has not abandoned Sarah, Gretchen, David, or me. He's been there taking every step with us. And God has not abandoned you or your loved one either. Do not let that lie stay in your mind. God has sent us His angels to support us and show His love for us. That's been God's provision for us all along and Jesus's direction for us since He walked the earth. Praise God!

chapter 7

God Is Our Father

In preparation for Daniel's memorial service, Sarah, Gretchen, David, and I all agreed that there was one picture of Daniel that best represented his journey, his life that was laid out before him, and the ultimate future God had in store for him. We decided to have it blown up and placed at the entrance to the church for the memorial service. The picture is of Daniel at a beach on a sunny, blue-skied summer day. His hand is shielding his eyes from the sun like a visor as he looks off into the distance. Look familiar? The picture became so representative of all the thoughts I desired to convey in the book that I decided to use it as this book's cover.

It's a simple picture that really doesn't highlight any of Daniel's features, gestures, or personality traits we all cherished. You can't see his kind, deep blue eyes, his inviting smile, or his quiet nature. What you can see, though, is a strong young man with his entire life in front of him. You can see all the hope that this life had for him.

Prior to Daniel's diagnosis, I caught a precious glimpse of that hope. One day out of the blue, while he was still wading through college trying to figure out what he wanted to do, Daniel asked me why I never encouraged him to go into engineering since my background was in engineering and his brother, David, was also an engineer. When he said that to me, I just about fell out of my chair in disbelief. In the past, Daniel had never expressed any interest in any kind of technical area, yet we knew that he was gifted in math. Without hesitation, I knew the perfect fit for him, so I encouraged him to enter an electrical engineering program, and he agreed. As soon as he started, he knew that this curriculum was a good fit for him, so he finally found the motivation needed to get his degree.

It warmed my heart to know that he would follow in my footsteps, but more importantly, that he was thinking about his future and was willing to commit to something he wanted. This was a turning point for his maturing from an adolescent into a man. I knew that making that commitment demonstrated a change in his thinking that would prepare him for whatever challenges stood before him.

What brought me even more joy was seeing the person he was becoming. Daniel had a quiet confidence. He knew that he would be successful in anything he set his mind to, yet he was also humble, kind, and caring. As a father, there's no greater joy than to see your son become the man you've always wanted him to be. All the years of nurturing and coaching were finally paying off as I witnessed my son's character development.

There was so much promise for Daniel's future, so after he left us, the knowledge that he would never reach his full potential here on earth hurt. I wanted him to be able to experience all the joys of this life. I wanted to see him as a dad, to see him have children and grandchildren. I wanted to watch his relationship with Sarah blossom as they grew old together. I wanted to help him though the difficulties he would face balancing his career and family.

It was painful knowing that those milestones would never be reached. The reality cut deep into my heart. I couldn't see how the pain could ever lessen or the wound heal because those opportunities were lost.

Maybe you can relate to this. Like me, you know in your head that the presence of God is a far better place for your loved ones than this earth, but you also see the joys of the God-created world and want them to experience those. You wonder, is that wrong? Is God frowning down on you for your desires? Can't He understand them?

God can and does understand. After all, He set this plan in motion in the first place. He understands the beginning from the end. It is we who lack in understanding. I believe our desire to hold on to this life stems from our lack of truly internalizing our relationship with God and what He intends for us. As God drew me back into His Word, it was this understanding that brought me peace and helped me to move forward.

94

God as a Father

As Jesus was spending time in prayer, His disciples asked Him how to pray, and He responded by giving us the Lord's Prayer. The very first thing Jesus wanted us to acknowledge and know about God is that He is our Father:

"Our Father in heaven, hallowed be Your name." (Lk 11:2)

There are countless passages in the Old and New Testaments that say the same. Isaiah tells us:

But now, O Lord,
You are our Father;
We are the clay, and You our potter;
And all we are the work of Your hand. (Isa 64:8)

God's being our Father is not an analogy. It is real, and it is truth. God is our Father. He loved us before we were born and ordained our paths (Ps 139:15–16). He created us in His image (Gen 1:26). He created us with the gifts and talents we have. He placed us in the families we have. He blesses us with unique circumstances and relationships. He works with each and every one of us to mold and shape our characters (Ps 33:15) so that we can be with Him and be a part of Him.

God knows each of us better than we know ourselves. He knows our thoughts before they enter our consciousness. He knows exactly what it will take to turn us back to Him. Therefore, His direction and instruction for each of us are uniquely and perfectly designed to do just that—to turn us back to Him so that we desire to be a part of Him.

Paul, in two separate letters, spoke of God's Spirit living within us and transforming us from our former selves into God's children. To explain our relationship with God, he uses the Aramaic word *abba*.

For you did not receive the spirit of bondage again to fear, but you received the Spirit of adoption by whom we cry out, "Abba, Father." (Rom 8:15)

And because you are sons, God has sent forth the Spirit of His Son into your hearts, crying out, "Abba, Father!" Therefore you are no longer a slave but a son, and if a son, then an heir of God through Christ. (Gal 4:6–7)

The word *abba* is best translated as *dad* or *daddy*. It was a word used by children to address their fathers. It represents that intimate, trusting relationship a child has with their dad. It represents our relationship with God. He is our dad. It's the same word that Jesus used on the night before His crucifixion as He prayed so intimately to the Father:

And He said, "Abba, Father, all things are possible for You. Take this cup away from Me; nevertheless, not what I will, but what You will." (Mk 14:36)

In the story of the prodigal son Jesus told, this image of God being our compassionate, loving Father is highlighted:

"There was a man who had two sons. The younger one said to his father, 'Father, give me my share of the estate.' So he divided his property between them.

"Not long after that, the younger son got together all he had, set off for a distant country and there squandered his wealth in wild living. After he had spent everything, there was a severe famine in that whole country, and he began to be in need. So he went and hired himself out to a citizen of that country, who sent him to his fields to feed pigs. He longed to fill his stomach with the pods that the pigs were eating, but no one gave him anything.

"When he came to his senses, he said, 'How many of my father's hired servants have food to spare, and here I am starving to death! I will set out and go back to my father and say to him: Father, I have sinned against heaven and against you. I am no longer worthy to be called your son; make me like one of your hired servants.' So he got up and went to his father.

"But while he was still a long way off, his father saw him and was filled with compassion for him; he ran to his son, threw his arms around him and kissed him.

"The son said to him, 'Father, I have sinned against heaven and against you. I am no longer worthy to be called your son.'

"But the father said to his servants, 'Quick! Bring the best robe and put it on him. Put a ring on his finger and sandals on his feet. Bring the fattened calf and kill it. Let's have a feast and celebrate. For this son of mine was dead and is alive again; he was lost and is found.' So they began to celebrate." (Lk 15:11–24 NIV)

God is a Father who wants close intimacy with His children. He knows we will stray from him, yet He is always there, waiting with open arms for us to come back to Him. When we do, His compassion and love toward us overflow as He warmly welcomes us back into His arms.

God our Father provides us with everything we need to sustain our lives. He provides us with every good gift we need (Jas 1:17). He directs our paths and comforts our hearts. He also, however, corrects our behavior:

Furthermore, we have had human fathers who corrected us, and we paid them respect. Shall we not much more readily be in subjection to the Father of spirits and live? For they indeed for a few days chastened us as seemed best to them, but He for our profit, that we may be partakers of His holiness. (Heb 12:9–10)

My son, do not despise the chastening of the Lord,
Nor detest His correction;
For whom the Lord loves He corrects,
Just as a father the son in whom he delights. (Prov 3:11–12)

While our human father corrects us to the best of his abilities and shapes our character to match his desires for us, God's correction is perfectly suited for us to prepare us for the future He has in store for us.

God loves us with a love that far exceeds the capacity of a human father's love (which, as any father knows, is huge).

All of this amounts to the truth that God wants us to know without any reservation that He is our Father. The disciples of Jesus knew how important this is to Him, so lest we forget, in almost every letter written in the New Testament, the disciples included an acknowledgment of God as our Father: "Grace to you and peace from God our Father and the Lord Jesus Christ" (1 Cor 1:3).

My Love versus God's

Let me pause here to say that I know you might not have a positive relationship with your father. Maybe you never had a father figure involved at all. With just about everything in this life, the human experiences we have provide us with insight into the spiritual reality God wants us to understand and embrace. Such is the case with our human fathers. By experiencing the love, provisions, and protections our human fathers provide for us, we can start to know the love and concern our ultimate Father has for us. Our adversary, however, has done everything in his power to keep us from this understanding. Breaking the family unit apart has been very effective in masking the true nature of God's love and destroying the very desire in some to be a part of a family unit. That is such a tragedy that will be corrected someday soon.

Being a father myself and being a part of a family with healthy relationships has blessed me with a good foundation for understanding God's love for us. It has helped me to understand how God desires to relate to us.

I was blessed with two boys whom I will always love dearly. They've meant everything to me. I was in love with them before they were born, while they were still a promise from God, and from the moment they were born, we had an unbreakable connection.

I can still vividly remember the days we took our sons home from the hospital. I have this mental picture of the day we took our oldest son home. There I was, standing next to Gretchen as she sat in our rocker holding David, both of us wondering what to do next as he peacefully slept while making soft sucking noises with his mouth. Needless to say, that moment didn't last very long, and his demands dictated our next steps. Gretchen and I were on our own with no family to support us and no experience caring for a newborn, so those first few months were wonderfully scary for us.

Starting off, I was still quite selfish with my time. While the boys were infants, there were many difficult days for me. (You moms out there will probably laugh at my laments.) I can remember how I hated when the weekends came because I was responsible for getting up through the night and feeding the baby while Gretchen tried to catch up on the much-needed sleep she had missed through the week. David would sleep two hours and take over an hour and a half to finish his bottle and go back to sleep. The lack of sleep and late-night infomercials really pulled me down. Then there were the colds, the ear infections, and the flare-ups of asthma that would make the boys sick and cranky (Mom and Dad too).

I will never forget one specific time. Just three months after David was born, my first trip to Japan for work was scheduled. I was to be there for four weeks. That on its own made it difficult for me to leave him and Gretchen. Then, the night before my flight departed, David had an asthma attack in the middle of the night. It was winter, so the doctor recommended that, before taking him to emergency, we put him in a warm shower, and if that didn't work, we take him outside briefly in the colder, dry air. The thought was that the changes in environment might calm the attack. So there I was, taking a shower with David at midnight, then taking him outside in the cold, and eventually taking him to emergency, all before getting on a plane a few hours later. I learned what love is all about that night, and it crushed me to be separated from my family.

So yes, those early days were difficult. Yet what a joy to see the boys gain motor skills and develop personalities. Our boys were totally dependent on us for everything. The bonds created in those years will last forever.

The young years that followed were a time when Dad was pretty special. The boys and I would do things together, and I could really see that they looked up to me and enjoyed spending time with me. I was blessed with the opportunity to mold their characters. It was during this time that I realized what it truly means to be Dad. If I was to be a role model for the boys, I had to walk the talk. As I worked to apply the character traits I desired to pass on to my boys, like honesty, kindness, and integrity, my lack of character in those areas became exposed, my own weaknesses and struggles magnified. But it was such a wonderful responsibility I was given by God. I was actually molding my sons' character! I found joy in the conversations we would have at the dinner table and at bedtime. Even the times they would get in trouble and needed correction became additional moments to teach and mold them.

There were times, however, when I just wasn't equipped to mold the boys in the ways I wanted. Both David and Daniel were shy and introverted. They inherited those traits from both Gretchen and me, so we knew exactly how they felt. It would break our hearts to have to leave them at preschool knowing how uncomfortable and out of place they felt. David would eventually grow out of it, but Daniel took much longer to feel comfortable in his skin and would only allow certain people to share in his life. Even though we knew how the boys felt, we weren't equipped to provide them with the skills to overcome their inwardness. Our hope in this situation was that our love for the boys with God's help would overcome all our inadequacies as parents.

As loving parents, we do everything we can to nurture and develop our children, but God is our perfect parent. God's love for us began before He created each and every one of us. We are unique and special to Him. He considered every detail of our lives as He planned our birth and then brought us into this life through our parents. He decided the gifts He would bless us with (e.g., physical looks and talents, intelligence, social status, personality traits) and the paths He would take us on to realize and use those gifts. Daily He watches over every step of our development, even assigning angels to care for us (Matt 18:10). As we take each step in life, He is there to bless the good behaviors and correct the bad behaviors through the trials He places in front of us. He knows where He is taking us, so we will get there. His plan for us is perfect and will be accomplished.

This intimate connection God has with us does not make us robots. Rather, it magnifies how much love our Father has toward us. If you look at the relationship loving parents have with their children, you see that they will do everything in their power to mold their character, yet they will accomplish this without breaking their children's spirits. How much more so with God. God knows each of us better than we know ourselves, so His correction for each of us is perfectly suited to bring about the changes He desires for us. With human fathers, this is impossible, but with God, all things are possible—remember?

God's judgments toward us are always tempered by His mercy and compassion for us. He knows our frame. He knows our weaknesses. There is nothing that we do that takes Him by surprise. He will never lash out in anger toward us, but He will correct us, and sometimes that correction is appropriately severe.

I did the best I could to develop my sons' character, but despite my best intentions, daily life wasn't anything like I had imagined it would be. I learned that my sons and I weren't perfect (I know, what a revelation!). They weren't the perfect model citizens I had envisioned, and I wasn't a perfect role-model father. I didn't take advantage of every coaching opportunity presented to me, nor was I very thorough when I did coach. Sometimes I needed to let Daniel and David make mistakes on their own and then live with the consequences. Too often, though, I bailed them out before the behavior was truly corrected. When I did correct them, my desire was to get everything out on the table quickly and then make sure our relationship remained intact by letting them know I loved them. Sometimes my anger would get the best of me, and I would do something I would soon regret. In those situations, I would struggle to swallow my pride and apologize. Yet I knew it was my responsibility to shape their character, and I often prayed for the strength of my own character to be there for my boys.

I failed my boys the most when they were young adults. As they were going through their high school years, I failed to realize that even though they were pushing me away to gain independence, they actually needed me more than ever. My desire to allow them to express themselves and make their own decisions resulted in me not addressing behaviors that were dangerous to them. I gave in to their desires too often and didn't speak up when I should have.

So I use my relationship with my sons to demonstrate how God feels toward us, but the reality of God's love is so much more far-reaching than human love can ever be. God is perfect, and His love for us and His judgments of us are also perfect. While I gave in to my sons' desires too often, God gives us exactly what we need, not what we request. Since God knows us so well, He is able to put consequences in front of us that will bring about the exact changes He wants in us. I may be selfish with my time or react out of emotion, but God is constant in His love and desire for us and will never, ever turn from us or leave us. I try to mold my sons into my image for them, yet God created each one of us with an outcome in mind that fits us perfectly. I may fail in molding my sons' character, but God will not fail and did not fail.

God was always there to guide my sons and be a bridge for my inadequacies. My sons both matured into wonderful men who love and cherish each other and their families. Their kindness and compassion humble me, and I am so thankful for God's help in raising them.

When Daniel passed away, as I've already mentioned, I was so preoccupied with knowing that he was okay, that he was being cared for and loved. Friends told me this was the father in me wanting to fulfill my responsibilities as Daniel's father. I knew they were right, but that didn't bring comfort to me. God had put Daniel in my care for twenty-six wonderful years and was now taking him back. I was actively involved with God's development of and care for Daniel those twenty-six years, so I was able to see firsthand how God was directing his every step. Why would God break that connection to Daniel when he passed away? Of course, the answer is He wouldn't. Daniel went back to God, into His loving arms, not into emptiness with no one to care for him. And yet that's how I was feeling. That's when God started reminding me of His tremendous love for Daniel, that He was Daniel's real Father.

The night before Jesus was to die, His close disciple John recorded a prayer between Him and our Father God. In this prayer, Jesus first talks about the relationship He has with our Father. His words reflect His loyalty and obedience to the Father and His acceptance of everything the Father asked Him to do. Jesus and our Father are perfectly aligned and support and complement each other. They both give of themselves to bring glory to the other and desire to be one with each other. They set a perfect example of love and service for all of us (Jn 17:1–5).

Jesus then goes on to pray for His disciples. He acknowledges that they belong to our Father, who gave them to Jesus to nurture and teach about Him. Jesus gave them everything the Father had for them, and they trusted that Jesus came from our Father and was one with Him. Now that Jesus is about to depart, He asks our Father to watch over them, care for them, protect them, and give them the joy that He has (Jn 17:6–19).

Finally, Jesus prays for all of us who would come to Him throughout the ages. He asks our Father to make us all one with Him as He and the Father are one with each other. He talks of the intimacy He desires with us, praying that we would be in Him just as He is in our Father. His desire for all of us, He says, is that we would be with Him where He is so that we may behold the glory given to Him by our Father and so that the love with which our Father loved Jesus may be in us:

> "I pray also for those who will believe in me through their message, that all of them may be one, Father, just as you are in me and I am in you. May they also be in us so that the world may believe that you have sent me. I have given them the glory that you gave me, that they may be one as we are one—I in them and you in me—so that they may be brought to complete unity. Then the world will know that you sent me and have loved them even as you have loved me.
>
> "Father, I want those you have given me to be with me where I am, and to see my glory, the glory you have given me because you loved me before the creation of the world." (Jn 17:20–24 NIV)

What a wonderful prayer! Jesus is asking our Father to make us one with Him and Jesus and bless us with the love that they share. He wants for us to be with Him, to be where He is so that we may see Him as He is in all the glory the Father has given Him. That's where Daniel is now and where I long to be also.

The problem wasn't that God left Daniel; the problem was that I wanted to hold onto Daniel. I didn't want to give Daniel back to God. As always, I wanted to control the situation. I wanted God to heal Daniel and provide him with all the things I thought were important for him to experience.

However, God's ways are different from the nature that He created in us, so there's a natural tension that exists. God wants us to trust in Him. He created us and therefore knows us better than we know ourselves. His wisdom transcends our thoughts, so we cannot even think to question Him, and yet we do ... continually. God doesn't want to take away our ability to reason, but He does desire to mold our character. Even God in the person of Jesus was unwilling to do anything apart from the Father. They had unity of thought and mind.

As I made my way through Daniel's journey with God, I was continually trying to control Him. If I needed to understand God's Word about healing, I would identify every verse and passage about healing. If faith was required, I had it. Whatever the requirement was, just let me know, and I would be there. Now, consciously, I didn't think I was trying to manipulate God, but as I reflect on what happened, I see that I couldn't allow myself to consider any verse or passage that told me I needed to give up all control of God's child, Daniel, and trust that His grace was sufficient for both of us.

Then, once Daniel was taken home, I needed God to justify why He allowed Daniel to get sick and why He took Daniel from us. I needed to know that God was going to take care of Daniel as well as I could. I needed to know that God loved Daniel. I needed confirmation that Daniel's life was not over but just beginning. Once again, without realizing it, I was trying to control God.

With all the demands I made and all my questioning of His decisions, God had every right, several times, to get angry and put me in my place. Even after He had brought comfort to me, I kept asking Him to give me the assurance that Daniel was okay, that he was being taken care of. Yet God in His grace, compassion, and love for me, being the loving Father that He is, slowly healed my heart and answered me in a subtle way that made me know that He was listening.

Daniel visited me in two dreams on separate occasions. The first time, I was in our kitchen, and Daniel and Sarah walked into the house with their normal greeting. As they walked into the kitchen, Daniel had a warm, inviting smile on his face. I immediately walked up to him and hugged him with an embrace that would not let go. I kept asking, "What's going on?" Daniel just kept smiling and gave me his familiar, affectionate coo. The dream ended with me waking up in tears. I tried to go back to sleep and resume the dream, but it was gone.

The second time, Daniel and I were somewhere on a high mountain looking out over the land. We were given a panoramic view of the world after God's kingdom had been well established. We both recognized how wonderfully beautiful the earth was and how the love for God and each other prevailed. I looked at him, and he smiled, in awe of it all.

These two dreams came to me at a time when I was being bombarded with negative thoughts about Daniel's care. I needed confirmation that Daniel was okay, so they helped me to fight off those negative thoughts. But God's most significant confirmation to us that Daniel was being cared for came from my sister-in-law, Sally. Two days after Daniel passed away, Sally had a dream about Daniel. He came to her with a beaming smile, looked directly at her, and addressed her as "Aunt Sally." What's unique here is that Daniel was always reserved and shy around relatives, so he very seldom if ever looked directly into anyone's eyes or addressed them by their name when greeting them. He would normally just say hi in passing.

He then asked Sally to tell us that he was so happy. Those were the words I was looking for all along; I was just looking for something that would assure me that he was okay and being cared for. The dream concluded by Daniel telling Sally that he had seen her mom and dad. They had passed away fifteen years prior.

There are two facts that made this confirmation so meaningful to me. Sally had no idea what I was struggling with, yet her dream brought the exact message I needed and at the right time. Interestingly enough, she wasn't able to tell us about her dream until months later. God brought her to us at a time when I was slipping back into a state of uncertainty over Daniel's care. Also, the dream didn't come from the immediate family—the people who needed it so desperately. In the midst of a trial, it's not always easy to discern whether or not something came from God and wasn't fabricated by our own desire. Whenever I seek God's direction, I look to confirm my understanding of His will through the council of others. Paul told the Corinthian church, "This will be the third time I am coming to you. 'By the mouth of two or three witnesses every word shall be established'" (2 Cor 13:1).

This approach to understanding God's will is not the only way we can know the direction or understanding came from Him, but it is a good rule of thumb. Having Sally bring this message to us when she did was exactly what I needed!

I once heard it said that God provides visions and dreams to those who are grieving and most in need of them. Thank you, Father, for that small but significant blessing you gave me.

God *Does* Care

As Daniel, Gretchen, and I would spend our evenings together studying scriptures on healing, we would also pray that God would bring someone into Daniel's life who would complete him. Not long after, Daniel met Sarah. The two of them were like two peas in a pod, perfectly suited for each other and connected in ways you don't typically find in loving married couples, much less people who just met and started dating. God clearly brought them together and made them equally yoked in their faith. On their first official date, they even staged a mock wedding ceremony.

Daniel and Sarah's first official date

Sarah immediately became part of the family and embraced Daniel's situation, trusting that God would carry the two of them through

106

whatever lay ahead. She started attending the quarterly oncologist visits and eventually took my place at the visits since they usually occurred midweek and it took a while to get to the hospital. Having Sarah in his life also made Daniel more responsible and motivated to do well in school. He built a wonderful path for his future with Sarah beside him.

As 2016 began, both Daniel and Sarah carried heavy workloads at college. Daniel was set to graduate in the spring, and they were planning to marry in August. We all wanted to wait until Daniel graduated, found a job, and got married before starting the cancer treatments, so that became our prayer, although we were ready to walk through that door whenever God decided it was time.

As it turned out, 2016 was a wonderful year for Daniel and Sarah. Daniel graduated with a bachelor of science degree in electrical engineering and started working the very next week for a large machine-building company. He had found his dream job as a controls engineer. He loved the work he was doing and the challenges it provided. Daniel and Sarah spent the summer preparing for their wedding and were married on August 20, 2016. They had a charming destination wedding on a beautiful inland lake in Northern Michigan and honeymooned in St. Thomas. Sarah was accepted into a doctorate program in audiology, so they decided to rent an apartment near campus. It was so wonderful to watch the two of them start their lives together with so much optimism.

Praying before the wedding

The wedding kiss

With this, all the special events we were hoping to experience before Daniel began treatment were past us. We were so thankful to God for allowing Daniel to experience the fullness this life has for us. This may sound cliché, but Sarah truly did complete Daniel. Sarah gave him confidence in himself and helped him to mature and come out of his shell. He now had purpose to his life. He had goals. He had someone to walk through this life with.

In the three and a half years that Daniel and Sarah were together, I witnessed the coming of age of my beloved son. He was no longer a young adult reluctant to take on the challenges of life. He was a man who embraced the challenges of life and desired a growing relationship with his Father. God knew the desires of our hearts for Daniel were good. He wanted those same things for Daniel, and so He blessed him with Sarah.

Through it all, God's hand in Daniel's life was evident, and I am so thankful for that. For a time, I may have lost sight of all that God was doing in and for Daniel. God allowed me to have time to grieve, and He showed compassion toward me when I was angry with Him. Yet He didn't let me stay there. His love has softened my heart and caused me to know that Daniel is being taken care of.

God will always want what's best for us, so you can trust that He will not abandon you or your loved one. Even though His ways are so far beyond what we can comprehend, He created this world for us and wants us to experience the fullness of life. In whatever your situation, God is there and is intimately involved and will listen to your heart. He may not give you all you ask for, but His plans for you and your loved one far exceed anything you can comprehend. In this I trust and rest.

chapter 8

And We Are His Children

One evening, Gretchen and I were watching a movie in which the mother of the main character passed away. At the funeral service, an acquaintance hugged the son and told him something along the lines of "Your mother lives on within us." The idea is a sentimental one that is meant to comfort, but it wasn't enough to comfort me. Keeping Daniel alive in my heart by holding on to memories of him was just an empty thought. Memories? That's it? I needed more. I needed to know that Daniel was okay, as I've already shared. I needed to know that Daniel was alive and being cared for. A sentimental thought could never satisfy that desire in me.

I found that I had the same reaction to friends and acquaintances who would tell me that Daniel was in a better place or that he was in heaven now. Those well-intended words were all but meaningless to me. There had to be a higher purpose for Daniel's life than being a bridge to some abstract place we refer to as heaven. All these expressions we use to bring comfort to others have their place, but I needed reassurance that our lives have meaning and purpose beyond our time here on earth.

As followers of Jesus, our typical message to the world and each other is that God will bless us with eternal life when we turn back to Him and recognize Him as our creator. If we're asked for more information, we include that eternal life means being with God in heaven. We can imagine what our destiny will be, but we seldom if ever really dig into and grasp all that God has for us. For those of us who have been walking with God for some time, we've learned and know that God is our Father. However, even for mature followers of our Lord, we will only take our relationship with Him so far. In our minds, there's God the Father, Jesus, and the Holy Spirit—the "Trinity," as we refer to God—and then there's us. We will be with God in heaven.

It's a good message that I don't mean to undermine or criticize. It emphasizes the nature of God, but that message on its own doesn't grasp our true destiny and what God is so wonderfully giving to us. The real gift freely given to us is to be God's family.

As we looked at in the previous chapter, God is our Father. I knew this well throughout the fight for Daniel's life and even after. What made the difference for me, though, was the realization that God's being our Father means we are His children.

This relationship is not just a metaphor used to describe a less significant relationship with God. If anything, the physical equivalents used to help us understand spiritual realities always fall short in expressing the fullness of what will actually be. They never represent a lesser spiritual equivalence. When God tells us that He is our Father and we are His children, our relationship with Him is fuller and more complete than what we will ever experience in our human family. We are given life and a spirit by God at birth and given His Spirit as we enter His family. His Spirit living in us makes us one with Him (Jn 17:21).

As a parent, needing to know that my son was being cared for meant everything to me. Once Daniel left this world, my ability to provide him with care and guidance was gone. I was forced to turn to God for the reassurance that everything would be okay. At that point, I realized that my understanding of God's plan for Daniel was too superficial to lean on and move forward with. But as God carried me back into His Word, the fullness of His intentions for us as His children was illuminated to me. This understanding brought me the peace and comfort I so desperately needed.

The questions or frustrations you have are almost surely different from what I experienced. However, the fundamental question is the same: how can you know with certainty that you and your loved ones will be greeted with joy and happiness as you leave this world?

You can know that because leaving this world is stepping into our destiny. Our destiny is to be sons of the Most High God (Lk 6:35). We will be in God's house, within God's walls, shining forth in the kingdom of our Father. We will be given names better than sons and daughters, for we will be given everlasting names that shall not be cut off (Isa 56:5; Matt 13:43). Through humankind, God is creating His family. Our ultimate destiny is to be God's family—to be the children of God.

A Common Destination

There are several places in the Old and New Testaments where our ultimate destiny is described as being the children of God, sons of God, sons of our Father, sons of the Most High, and sons of the living God. It's a theme that runs throughout the scriptures, but I want to take us deeper than just the concept of being God's children. I want us to explore what God truly intends for us and reveals to us about our destiny.

Our discussion starts with God's intentions for us when He created humankind.

> Then God said, "Let Us make man in Our image, according to Our likeness." (Gen 1:26)

In the creation story, God tells us that we were made in His image and likeness. In Hebrew, the word translated *image* conveys that the likeness of God is expressed in us—that is, that we are very similar to God.

When trying to unravel what this means, we typically identify parallels between ourselves and God in our ability to reason and capacity to love, think, feel, will, and speak. These are all good characteristics that help us understand our relationship to God; however, if we step back a bit, we see something even more wonderful being conveyed to us in this passage.

Looking at the genealogy of Adam as it is given to us, the words *image* and *likeness* are used to describe a son born to Adam and Eve:

> And Adam lived one hundred and thirty years, and begot a son in his own likeness, after his image, and named him Seth. (Gen 5:3)

Seth was made in his father's image and likeness. This doesn't mean that Seth was Adam—of course not—but that his son was born of humankind. So when God created man in His image and likeness, was He creating man from the Godkind? Was God's intention from the very beginning to actually reproduce Himself when He created man?

David alluded to this in the Psalms. David was a man after God's own heart. He loved God and looked to Him for all his needs and desires. Yet David was also human, with human weaknesses that brought on correction from God. As he would pray to God, he would often meditate on God's plan for humankind. In Psalm 17, he states:

> As for me, I will see Your face in righteousness;
> I shall be satisfied when I awake in Your likeness. (Ps 17:15)

David's meditation ends by looking beyond death to his eventual awakening to the satisfaction of being in God's likeness. Even though David recognized all his shortcomings, he knew that his destiny was not going to end with this physical existence we have here. He knew we were meant for more than any other created beings. He knew that our destiny was to live on and to be like God.

Peter expounds on this thought by telling us that God's divine power has given us all things pertaining to life and godliness:

> Grace and peace be multiplied to you in the knowledge of God and of Jesus our Lord, as His divine power has given to us all things that pertain to life and godliness, through the knowledge of Him who called us by glory and virtue, by which have been given to us exceedingly great and precious promises, that through these you may be partakers of the divine nature, having escaped the corruption that is in the world through lust. (2 Pet 1:2–4)

God has given us an exceedingly great and precious promise. We will be partakers of His divine nature. Wait. Let me restate that claim so that we can all grasp the fullness of God's gift to us. *We will partake of God's divine nature!*

Paul gives us more insight into what God's intention was in giving us His divine nature. When he traveled to Athens, he was asked to speak in front of all the educated men there. Paul, seeing an altar with an inscription, "TO THE UNKNOWN GOD," used this as an opportunity to introduce the men to our Creator God. Paul's short presentation is an amazing summary of the majesty of God and our relationship with Him.

Paul first and foremost identifies God as the creator of everything in the heavens and on the earth. He rejects the notion that God needs any place to dwell or human representation or activity for worship since He is above all we can make or imagine. God is life, so anything that has life comes from Him. He gives life to all things.

Paul then explains that our attention should be toward God. We should seek Him and pursue Him even though He is never far from us:

> For in Him we live and move and have our being, as also some of your own poets have said, "For we are also His offspring." Therefore, since we are the offspring of God, we ought not to think that the Divine Nature is like gold or silver or stone, something shaped by art and man's devising. (Act 17:28–29)

God provides for and sustains our lives because we're His offspring, and we become His offspring by His allowing us to partake of His divine nature. Therefore, we shouldn't consider the divine nature to be anything we've devised or created. As I mentioned earlier, it's God's Spirit living in us that makes us one with Him (Jn 17:21), so we should always look at God's plan for us with humility and awe over what He will accomplish through us.

Do you see where God is leading us and what He wants us to understand about our relationship with Him? Just saying that we are the children of God is difficult to connect with because we are human and can't comprehend spiritual matters. Besides that, our reasoning makes our Father God and a human child of God incompatible ideas. There is God, who is a Spirit and is infinitely above us, and then there is us, in all our frailty as humans, yet we're somehow His children.

John addresses these conflicting thoughts by telling us:

> Behold what manner of love the Father has bestowed on us, that we should be called children of God! Therefore the world does not know us, because it did not know Him. Beloved, now we are children of God; and it has not yet been revealed what we shall be, but we know that when He is revealed, we shall be like Him, for we shall see Him as He is. And everyone who has this hope in Him purifies himself, just as He is pure. (1 Jn 3:1–3)

We may not be able to grasp all that God has in store for us yet, but that doesn't change the reality of what God will accomplish through us. On the day we stand before God, we shall see Him as He is because we will be like Him.

Just before His crucifixion, Jesus prayed for us in a way that drives this point home. He prayed that we would be one with Him, just as He is one with the Father.

> "I in them, and You in Me; that they may be made perfect in one, and that the world may know that You have sent Me, and have loved them as You have loved Me." (Jn 17:23)

God's Spirit is not separate from us. His Spirit becomes a part of us, and when it does, we are grafted into God's family. His Spirit unites with our spirit to make us His children, His family. We are not a part of God's family in the way that your beloved pet is a part of your family; we are made in the image of God and take on the fullness of His character through His Spirit. We are one with God.

Paul went through a tremendous amount of suffering after he was called into service by God. He knew we would also experience suffering, so he wanted us to be able to look beyond the conditions we find ourselves in today—the sicknesses, suffering, failings of ourselves and our societies—to the awesome future that stands before us.

> For I consider that the sufferings of this present time are not worthy to be compared with the glory which shall be revealed in us. For the earnest expectation of the creation eagerly waits for the revealing of the sons of God. For the creation was subjected to futility, not willingly, but because of Him who subjected it in hope; because the creation itself also will be delivered from the bondage of corruption into the glorious liberty of the children of God. (Rom 8:18–21)

Looking beyond our physical life to the time when we are liberated children of God was hard for me to do after Daniel passed away. I could never have pulled myself away from the grief were it not for God's love for me and for Daniel. Knowing that God loved Daniel enough to make him His child and that he had received God's divine nature gave me the peace and comfort I was longing for. It's what we all need to hold on to in our time of suffering or loss. All of God's creation eagerly waits for humankind to step into our ultimate destiny as God's children.

I have a family. There's me and Gretchen, my wife, and our children, David and Daniel. We are all Pouliots. We are united in the family unit that carries our name. I am a Pouliot, Gretchen is a Pouliot, David is a Pouliot, and Daniel is a Pouliot. We are all proud of our heritage and represent the Pouliot family in everything we do. When the boys were young, I used to remind them that they were Pouliots, so their actions were a reflection on all of us. The same is true of our relationship with God.

Our destiny through God's grace is to be His children, His family, His heirs, and joint heirs with Christ (Rom 8:17). We take on His name. We were made in His image and take on His divine nature when His Spirit joins with ours. God's love for us as our Father is shown to us by the fact that we are His children.

Heaven

I may have been sensitive to people making comments about Daniel's going to heaven, but there is a reason why so many people bring this up to someone grieving. What happens to us after death is a relevant part of life, yet our understanding of that time is confusing to most and somewhat masked from us. Because of this, we typically package this time in a neatly framed concept called "heaven." We use the concept of heaven to encapsulate all that happens to us once we leave this time and place.

As I worked my way through the grieving process, I never questioned what it will be like in God's kingdom. My thoughts would always take me to that moment when I will be able to look Daniel in the eyes, hear his voice again, and hug him without letting go. It seems like the thoughts of everyone grieving over the loss a loved one go to this place. However, given all that we've already explored and our individual understandings of God, we might feel a sense of guilt over this.

Being reunited with loved ones doesn't seem like an appropriate first thought about heaven, does it? Why is it that we think this way? Shouldn't our thoughts of going to heaven be centered on the knowledge that we will finally be face-to-face with our Creator God and see Him as He is? Shouldn't the greatest realization of heaven be that we are one with God and members of His family?

I don't think it's wrong for us to be comforted more by the thought of being reunited with loved ones than by being in the presence of God. I do believe God allows for this. After all, our loved ones were physically with us in some cases for many, many years, and we will not fully know God until we are with Him, as John tells us:

> Beloved, now we are children of God; and it has not yet
> been revealed what we shall be, but we know that when
> He is revealed, we shall be like Him, for we shall see Him
> as He is. (1 Jn 3:2)

It's difficult to truly know what lies beyond this life, especially when we're grieving over the loss of a loved one. Years ago, I heard a minister describe our understanding of what stands before us using the analogy of an unborn child still in his mother's womb. It's stayed with me all these years. Prior to Daniel's passing, I would refer to it whenever I ran into someone who questioned life beyond death. After Daniel left us, though, I needed to remind myself of it.

The unborn child lives in the comfort and security of his own little world. He's kept warm, protected from danger, and provided all the food and nourishment required to survive and grow. The child hears sounds and perceives light and darkness from the world outside his mom, but he has no concept of what's actually out there. The child doesn't want to leave the environment that he's grown up in and knows so well. When he enters the world, he comes in screaming.

The unborn child cannot comprehend what waits for him outside Mommy. And even if there were a way for us to communicate to him what the outside world is like, he doesn't have the experience, intellect, or maturity to understand. Imagine trying to explain playing at the park with friends, or going to school, or meeting that special someone and getting married. All the things we cherish and love as humans could never be comprehended by this little child. He wouldn't be able to connect any of the dots because he's never experienced anything outside his mother. Besides, why would the child ever want to leave the place that provides for all his needs?

That's how it is for us now. We can only comprehend what we know and see, what we've experienced and know to be possible. We struggle to imagine that there is anything that awaits us after we die. To think that what's ahead is even more wonderful than what we have here is difficult, so we use things familiar to us to help fill in the blanks and give us something concrete to hold on to. This includes the thought of being with our loved ones who have gone before us. We also frequently imagine what it will be like with no more sorrow or pain, or growing old, or hatred and violence. We look at the failings of society and consider what the world will be like when God's ways are the rule of law.

Yet God tells us that our future is so much better than what we can comprehend or have now.

> But as it is written:
> "Eye has not seen, nor ear heard,
> Nor have entered into the heart of man

The things which God has prepared for those who love Him." (1 Cor 2:9)

I meditated on this promise from God and was drawn to know what it was like in that moment when Daniel passed from this life into the next. God doesn't give us much detail about what it will be like when we are finally standing before Him, probably because there is so much we wouldn't comprehend, like the little infant inside his mother's womb. However, that precious time is not completely veiled from us.

God does tell us about His nature and how He manifests Himself to us. The Bible tells us that the essence of God's character is love. We've already discussed how we can know and experience God's love for us. Any act of love toward us or by us comes from God. We are also given a glimpse of what we will encounter as we stand before Him. God's expression of Himself to us, what we will experience when we are in His presence, is light.

> This is the message which we have heard from Him and declare to you, that God is light and in Him is no darkness at all. (1 Jn 1:5)

The Bible consistently uses light to describe God's presence as He manifests Himself to us. Using Paul's first encounter with Jesus again, the glory of His presence blinded Paul. Recounting his experience later, Paul would describe the presence of Jesus this way:

> While thus occupied, as I journeyed to Damascus with authority and commission from the chief priests, at midday, O king, along the road I saw a light from heaven, brighter than the sun, shining around me and those who journeyed with me. (Act 26:12–13)

Consider our understanding of light. Light in its purest form, white light, contains a complete range of all the colors of the spectrum. Over the ages, white objects have symbolized purity to us. Light illuminates and warms. Light provides the energy to sustain life and promote growth. Without light, there would be no life.

God's expression of Himself to us as light helps us to understand the purity, righteousness, and absolute holiness of His character. God's light provides direction and guidance to us. Our life emanates from His light (Jn 8:12). When we are standing in the presence of God, we will need for nothing else.

> "The sun shall no longer be your light by day,
> Nor for brightness shall the moon give light to you;
> But the Lord will be to you an everlasting light,
> And your God your glory.
> Your sun shall no longer go down,
> Nor shall your moon withdraw itself;
> For the Lord will be your everlasting light,
> And the days of your mourning shall be ended." (Isa 60:19–20)

My heart's desire is to be in Daniel's presence and embrace him when I leave this world. That will happen, but it will pale in comparison to God's loving embrace. I will be surrounded by God's love and His light.

I remember the first time I heard the song "I Can Only Imagine" by MercyMe shortly after it was released. I was working out on the front porch of my house and had the radio on. As soon as the first verse was over and I was able to understand the meaning of the song, I wept. Now, that's not me at all. In the past, I would never have let my emotions get away from me like that. My reaction surprised me.

For those of you who may not be familiar with the song, it questions how we will react at the moment we are in the presence of God. This beautiful song leaves you contemplating what you will do in that wonderful moment.

As I pondered why I became so emotionally affected by the song, I came to the realization that it really wasn't me who was driving this emotion. I had no idea what being in God's presence will be like and seldom, if ever, thought about it. Those emotions came from deep within me. It was God's Spirit that stirred me up and made me feel this way. At the time, my senses were overwhelmed with humility, gratitude, and praise for the mercy and compassion He had on me. Even though the song doesn't answer the question of what it will be like in God's presence, I got a glimpse of how I will feel in that moment.

My prayer is that you are able to use the insight God's Word and His Spirit provide you to truly know that the moment you and your loved ones are in God's presence will be like no other. When you move from this life into the next, you will be in the presence of God, surrounded by His light and love. What an amazing destiny we have standing before us, the door to which Daniel has already walked through.

You see, Daniel didn't die. He has moved on and goes before us. Daniel has already experienced that precious moment of being in the presence of God. He will forevermore live in the light and love of our Father God. How can I feel anything but joy for Daniel? How can I not long for that precious time myself?

Daniel was given to us for twenty-six wonderful years to provide for him and nurture him while God worked on his character. When God brought him to the place and time at which he had fulfilled all that He had for Daniel here, He took him back home. Daniel's life is not finished or complete. Daniel has eternity before him to continue to grow and mature as a child of God. Daniel is one with our Father God and Jesus.

Daniel John Pouliot was the name given to our son when he came into this world. We gave it to him because both Daniel and John were prominent biblical names and because we had a special connection with the name Daniel. Gretchen had been engaged to a young man with that name who tragically passed away, so giving Daniel his name was a way for us to honor his memory. God has given Daniel a new name now, though (Isa 62:2), an eternal name better than that of a son:

> "Even to them I will give in My house
> And within My walls a place and a name
> Better than that of sons and daughters;
> I will give them an everlasting name
> That shall not be cut off." (Isa 56:5)

God has given Daniel a name that represents his character. A name that represents his kindness, gentleness, and love of God and His Word. A name that represents Daniel's place within the family of God. A name that is written in His Book of Life (Phil 4:3). Oh, how I long to know that name!

Sheep of the Shepherd

Of all the examples of God being our Father and us being His children, there's one specific psalm of David that has been a treasure to me for many years. In it, David refers to God as his Shepherd. It's special to me because it portrays how God will guide and carry me through all the difficulties of this life:

> The Lord is my shepherd;
> I shall not want.
> He makes me to lie down in green pastures;
> He leads me beside the still waters.
> He restores my soul;
> He leads me in the paths of righteousness
> For His name's sake.
> Yea, though I walk through the valley of the shadow of death,
> I will fear no evil;
> For You are with me;
> Your rod and Your staff, they comfort me.
> You prepare a table before me in the presence of my enemies;
> You anoint my head with oil;
> My cup runs over.
> Surely goodness and mercy shall follow me
> All the days of my life;
> And I will dwell in the house of the Lord
> Forever. (Ps 23)

Applied to my life, this psalm tells me that I will never want for anything because God will always be there for me. All the goodness and blessings in my life come from Him and Him alone. He directs my path, so my thoughts should be outwardly focused on the needs of others.

I will go through difficult trials in my life, but I will never fear death or evil because my Father is with me. I clung to the knowledge that God would never leave me during Daniel's trials. I needed God there. The weight of what stood before me was too much for me to bear alone. Even when God did not answer my prayers in the way I wanted Him to and I was mad at Him, I still needed to know that He was there beside me.

Regardless of my actions, God's mercy will follow me all the days of my life because I dwell in my Father's house forever. I am a child of God who has an eternal destiny with my loving Father.

And now that Daniel has gone before me, I know that he will never want for anything either. God was with him through every step he took in this life. I saw God's love for him and witnessed His provisions for Daniel. Daniel had many challenges that he faced in life, yet God was always there to give him the strength he needed to endure every trial. I was blessed to see Daniel's faith blossom with God's guidance.

God has not abandoned Daniel. God was standing there waiting for him as he left his temporary dwelling. God was there to comfort and embrace him as He carried him forward to the next chapter in his life.

As you make your way through the trial that has been placed before you, there will be times of peace and comfort and times of despair. Your walk with God, however strong it is, will not eliminate these waves of uncertainty you experience. Always remember, though, that God is there with you. He is the same yesterday, today, and forever. He is there when doors are opened and peace and comfort abound, and He's there with you when doors slam shut and the spiritual attacks occur. He doesn't want you to feel abandoned. He is still there, still in control, and He still has you and your loved ones' best interests in mind.

Always know that God's goodness and mercy shall be with you regardless of what happens because you and your loved ones are His children. May this psalm bless you with comfort and peace as you journey with God through the trials of life.

chapter 9

Precious in His Sight

At this point in time, I'm able to reflect on Daniel's trials with a little more clarity. As I reflect on our walk with God, what stands out the most to me is the realization that I was unable to give up control over Daniel's life. You've surely seen that as a common theme throughout this book. His life was so, so dear to me. I wasn't consciously thinking that I was going to hold on to control and refuse to give Daniel over to God. I knew that was wrong. My mind just wouldn't even raise the thought of placing him in God's hands because it was too difficult.

I am now, however, able to see that my actions were clearly focused on controlling the outcome. I was going to do everything in my power to keep Daniel alive. It wasn't until God had taken every option away from me and it was clear that Daniel was gone that I finally thanked God for all the wonderful memories He gave me with Daniel and asked Him to take care of him. God had finally broken through my resistance to trusting Him.

God didn't break me down and leave me there. He has since picked me up by correcting my view of death. He has opened my mind to so much joy and promise for Daniel's future. Psalm 116:15 is a verse that I love and hold on to because it tells me that Daniel is okay because he's with his loving Father. And I like to insert Daniel's name at the end. That makes it so much more meaningful to me.

Precious in the sight of the Lord is the death of His [son Daniel].

The word translated as *precious* in this verse refers to something of great value, highly esteemed or cherished. In the midst of my grief, this told me that contrary to how I was feeling, God viewed this time in Daniel's life as a cherished, precious time. Daniel was home where God intended him to be from the beginning.

If you have lost a loved one, meditate on this verse, inserting their name. Ask God to bless you by giving you insight into His perspective on their life and His plans for them.

Precious in the sight of the Lord is the death of His [son/ daughter _____].

God loves your loved one more than you can comprehend and has planned for the time of their return to Him from before they were even born. He has watched over their life and brought them to this place. If this is the time He has planned to take them home, know how precious this time truly is! It's us and not God who holds on to the sting of death.

Grieving

Although all of what we have discussed is true, death still puts us in a state of grief over our loss. We all need to grieve. Grieving is a time for us to transition to the new reality that stands before us as we find our way after losing an integral part of us. What we don't need, though, is to have our hearts anchored to despair as if we have no hope for the future. So let's talk a little about grieving and then look at God's purpose in death.

When I spoke at Daniel's memorial service, I began by acknowledging to everyone that I wouldn't be talking to them about what Daniel meant to me. My words would never have been able to express the feelings I had for Daniel, nor would they have been able to paint a portrait of Daniel that encapsulated all the beauty of his personality. I'm still not able speak fully on these things. The twenty-six years I was blessed with Daniel are too intimate and hurt too much to share, at least for now.

I spoke of Daniel's faith in God, how his life changed after he became sick, although I didn't spend much time there. Daniel's faith blossomed, especially after God brought Sarah into his life. Sarah and Daniel were equally yoked in their love for God.

Daniel loved listening to Ravi Zacharias tapes and would read his books along with books by John Lennox. He wasn't really into defending his beliefs to others, but he was very logical in his reasoning, so he was able to connect with both Ravi and John. They helped to quench his thirst for God's Word.

I mentioned next that I was looking at things from my perspective, that I wanted God's promises here and now. I was consumed by my loss, but I knew God didn't want me to get stuck in that place. God was challenging me to look at the bigger picture. I acknowledged that Daniel never really belonged to me. He had always belonged to God. He is God's child whom I was blessed to nurture for twenty-six wonderful years. God loves Daniel more than I could ever love him. He doesn't want less than I wanted for Daniel; He wants so much more than I could even imagine.

I concluded by saying that Daniel had gone before us and that I was so proud of his courage and faith. I brought everyone back to the picture of Daniel standing on a beach, looking out over the water. That far-off place that Daniel was looking toward is the place where I also longed, and still long, to be. It represented the time when we leave this earthly tent we live in and take on the eternal body that God has prepared for us. It represented being with our loving Father.

"As long as I'm on this earth," I told our friends and family, "I will long for the day when I see Daniel again and we are brothers in our Father's family. So then, I will rest in God's love for Daniel and look forward to our family reunion."

Those are the words I spoke and the message I wanted to convey and believe. At the time, though, the grief was too strong to truly believe what I was saying. We all need to grieve, and for each of us, the grieving process is different. So far in my lifetime, I've lost my father, my father-in-law, my mother-in-law, and a few aunts I was close to. Those times were painful for me, but just knowing that God loved them, that they were in a better place, and that I would soon be reunited with them made it relatively easy for me to let go of them and continue to move forward with my life.

But Daniel's situation was different. The grieving and loss were profound. Being a father and watching the life of someone I loved as dearly as Daniel slip away at such a young age made me question all those things I was trusting in. In the days after Daniel's memorial service, I couldn't find peace. I had so many questions that I needed answers to. I wanted to talk to Daniel. I wanted to tell him that I loved him and missed spending time with him. I wanted to ask him if he was okay. I wanted him to forgive me for not protecting him or reacting to his condition sooner and getting him the right care. I wanted his forgiveness for letting him down so many times. I wanted to ask him if he had seen and talked to God yet.

The person we are is shaped in large part by the people who touch our lives, especially those with whom we are intimate. We draw much of our identity from these special people. As soon as Daniel was gone, I felt the void in me. A significant part of me had been taken away, and he was not surgically removed with minimal damage; he was torn out. I felt as though my being was left in tatters. The person I was before no longer existed. For me to move forward, I had to accept that—that I would never be the same. Grieving gave me the time I needed to figure out who this new me was.

Don't put any expectations on yourself to get over the grief. The path is not linear. There's no five-step process to moving on. In fact, I reject the notion that I will ever move on from this. The pain and loss will always be there. I will never be the person I was before. But with God's help, I will move forward with my life, and I will embrace this new reality ... someday.

Grieving is a natural process that we all need to go through and doesn't reflect on our maturity as followers of Jesus. In the story of Lazarus, Jesus knew that if He waited to go see Lazarus, he would be dead. He wanted that to happen because He wanted everyone to know that He had power over death, the power to resurrect the dead to life. He knows all the wonderful things that are planned for His creation, so He knew that death was not the end but the beginning.

Yet when Jesus came to Lazarus's tomb and saw how everyone was grieving, He wept. Not because He was concerned for Lazarus but because He knew the emotions the family and friends were experiencing and had compassion on them for their loss. In fact, Jesus tells us that we are blessed when we mourn because we will be comforted (Matt 5:4). Grieving is an important component of our moving forward after losing someone. Grief is an emotion ordained by God that will ultimately bring us peace and comfort.

God is not distant from us when we grieve. He is right there with us, helping us through each and every breath we take. He cares for us and is with us with every tear we shed.

> You number my wanderings;
> Put my tears into Your bottle;
> Are they not in Your book? (Ps 56:8)

Always remember that God loves you more than you can comprehend. He holds on to every memory of you—the good, the bad, the joyous, and the sad. They are all important to Him. He captures every memory just like we hold on to photographs and videos of our loved ones. Grieving is difficult for us, yet it is precious for God because it draws us into Him.

One more thought on grieving. I feel compelled to identify a method our adversary uses to keep us captive in our grief and turn us against our Father. As I mentioned earlier, my grief started out as waves that would overwhelm me. As time went on, the grief came in the form of flashbacks. What triggered the flashbacks was always different. I might have seen a picture of Daniel or run into someone close to Daniel or taken part in an event that brought back special memories, such as Thanksgiving or his birthday. What was common was where the flashbacks would ultimately take me. It was always a place of intense pain—thoughts of Daniel's suffering in his last days, of being there with him during his last few hours, of lost opportunities to make new memories with him, or just of the reality that he was gone, that he was dead. All those hurtful thoughts would crash over me and bury me in sorrow. Those thoughts were continually being broadcasted in my mind by our adversary.

But God was always there to rescue me. He would continually bring me back to His Word and His promises for us. When our adversary would remind me of Daniel's pain, God would whisper to me that He had taken away any pain or suffering Daniel experienced. When I was reminded that Daniel was dead, God would tell me that that was a lie. Daniel is not dead; he is alive and with the one who loves him more than words can express. When I was reminded that there would be no more memories to make, God would proclaim to me that I will have an eternity of memories to make with Daniel and all my family members.

This is my prayer for any of you who are currently grieving—that you will call on God and allow Him to replace any painful attacks and lies our adversary communicates to you with the truth of what our loving Father has in store for you and your loved one. Do not let our adversary keep you in despair. Realize what's happening and let God defend you.

> Precious in the sight of the Lord is the death of His [son/daughter _____].

God's Purpose in Death

I started this journey with Daniel desiring to bring praise to God through his healing. In my limited understanding, I simply couldn't imagine how God could ever be glorified through the premature death of my son. Besides, that wasn't the outcome I desired, so why even go there? I really didn't give it much consideration at all because my heart wouldn't let me. Daniel would be miraculously healed, and everyone would see God's hand in it.

However, that's not what God wanted. Instead, He wanted me to be able to see the depth and width and breadth of His love for Daniel, my son and His child. He wanted me to proclaim His wonder and majesty to everyone. He wanted me to talk of His love for all of us—a love that will not be denied or quenched, not even in death.

You see, it was never my responsibility to decide how to bring glory to God. I'm not capable of knowing God's character well enough to speak for Him, nor should I ever feel as though His actions need to be justified. That's how I was behaving, though, similarly to Job. Job wanted answers from God. He wanted to know why God brought such suffering upon him. He wanted to justify himself before God. But then God corrected him for questioning His actions, and he responded with a much humbler yet mature understanding of God and His ways. Job told God that he knew that nothing was impossible for Him, so whatever He purposed would be done. He recognized that he really didn't understand God's ways because they were too wonderful for him to know. He realized that he could never question the works or intentions of his Creator (Job 42:1–6).

I was focused on bringing glory to God through Daniel's life. I thought that healing Daniel would magnify His love for him and all of us. Yet God wanted me to magnify His love for Daniel through his death. What God revealed to me was that I was deceiving myself. It wasn't that I had this unquenchable desire to bring praise to God. On the contrary, my true intention was to do whatever had to be done to save Daniel's life. Bringing praise to God was a way for me to control the situation. I was doing everything I could to prevent Daniel's death, while death is the one thing in life that we have absolutely no control over.

The story of Adam and Eve provides us with a powerful lesson about our nature, about our drive for control. When God allowed Adam and Eve to be influenced by our adversary, they immediately decided for themselves what was right and wrong. Their actions demonstrated the hostility we have toward God's control over our lives (Rom 8:7). The consequence of their rebellion, of our rebellion, is death.

Left to ourselves, we will always do things our way and reject what God teaches us. Our nature demands that we control our environment. The irony in all of this is that the one thing we demanded, control, was the very thing that was taken away from us by our actions. We have absolutely no control over death. It happens. It happens to all of us. We are all appointed to die once. No one can escape that judgment (Heb 9:27).

God's plan from the beginning was for us to have eternal life. That is what the tree of life represented in the garden of Eden. God told Adam and Eve that they could freely eat of that tree. However, once they rebelled against God, He took away their access to that tree (Gen 3:22–24).

That didn't, however, take away the God-given human desire to live forever.

> He has made everything beautiful in its time. Also He has put eternity in their hearts, except that no one can find out the work that God does from beginning to end. (Eccl 3:11)

God created a natural tension within us and between Himself and us. We have a need for control over our lives and our environment, but we also, more than anything else, desire to live on. The only way we can have eternal life is to come to Him. He and only He can give us the desire of our hearts, but we must come to Him for that gift.

> "For God so loved the world that He gave His only begotten Son, that whoever believes in Him should not perish but have everlasting life." (Jn 3:16)

It's not that God is trying to beat us into submission by holding such a precious gift over our heads and is unwilling to give us what we want unless we cave in and submit to Him. He has that power over us, but that's not His nature or His desire for us. God wants us to love Him. He wants us to recognize that life emanates from Him; He is life (Jn 1:4). He wants us to know His love for us. He wants us to know that we are His children and He will do whatever it takes to bring us back to Him. His love for us is so strong that He came to us as a man and died for us.

The Bible tells us very little about the experience of death. There are varying interpretations of the passages that relate to this and cases of near-death experiences that some of us use to fill the void, but for the most part, death is an unknown to us, so we fear it. We fear the moment of death. We fear what lies ahead. Our faith in God and what He tells us about death are all we have, and that's exactly where God wants us to be. God has purposely kept a veil over our understanding.

> Jesus said to her, "I am the resurrection and the life. He who believes in Me, though he may die, he shall live. And whoever lives and believes in Me shall never die. Do you believe this?" (Jn 11:25–26)

Death is always hanging over our heads. We push it to the back of our minds, but it always comes to the forefront whenever there is a tragedy we hear of or are forcefully thrust into. Death is a form of bondage we live in as long as we keep ourselves separated from God. And that's exactly where our adversary wants us to stay. He wants us to fear death. He wants us to question what lies ahead. And most importantly, he wants to drive a wedge between us and God with the matter of death.

Our adversary causes us to question what can be gained through death. Why would a loving God take someone with so much life in front of them? Why would God allow such a senseless death? Why would God allow death at all? That's where I was. I couldn't see why God would take Daniel from all the life he had in front of him, like having children and grandchildren and growing old with Sarah. These questions, though, take our eyes off God and mask God's true purpose in death. Don't allow our adversary to keep you there.

God uses death to draw us back to Him because He is the only source of life. Through Him we have the wonderful news that Jesus died for us and rose from the dead. His sacrifice for us allows us to be one with Him in His family as His children. God takes away our bondage to death (Heb 2:14–15), so that death is swallowed up in victory, allowing us to proclaim:

> "O Death, where is your sting?
> O Hades, where is your victory?" (1 Cor 15:55)

When God's plans for us have reached their fullness, "the last enemy that will be destroyed is death" (1 Cor 15:26).

These are all amazing revelations that we need to be firmly grounded in. God has made a way for us to say that death no longer has control over us. God puts death before us, yes. But He also made it so that through Him, through the death and resurrection of Jesus the Anointed One, we live. Death cannot keep us in bondage. We have victory over death. We do not die; we live. Your loved ones are alive.

> "A little while longer and the world will see Me no more,
> but you will see Me. Because I live, you will live also. At
> that day you will know that I am in My Father, and you
> in Me, and I in you." (Jn 14:19–20)

What makes God's plan for us even more wonderful is the promise that what stands before us is a life that is even better than what we currently have. As Paul addressed questions the Corinthian church had regarding the resurrection, he provided them and us with a comparison between what we leave and what we receive as our lives move forward. He tells us that what awaits us is an incorruptible spiritual body, raised in glory and power (1 Cor 15:42–45).

Living through the death of a loved one is one of the most difficult tests of your faith you can endure. In the days after Daniel's death, God kept putting in my heart that it's not about me or my hurt; it's about what God has done for us through Jesus. I was so focused on the pain and loss that I couldn't understand where God was taking me. As the fog cleared, though, I was able to see that death brings glory to God through what He's already done for us. God so loved us that He gave us His Anointed One, Jesus, to die for us so that death would be destroyed by life—His life. And because He lives, we will not die but will also live.

The tears I've cried have been tears of loss for the intimacy I once had and desire to have now with Daniel. I miss Daniel. I miss spending time with him. I miss our talks. I miss his voice. Yet God tells me that there will be a day when all my tears and the tears of all of His children will be wiped away because God through Jesus has swallowed up death forever (Isa 25:8). Death is a lie, a deception to keep us from the amazing truth of our destiny.

We have a God who is love and in love created us to be His offspring, His children. When we leave this world, our physical bodies will die because they were only ever meant to be temporary dwellings. But we live. We live with our God and Father. We are sons of God. I am able to stand before you now and confidently proclaim that my son is not dead but alive because of all that God has already done for him and for all of us through the death and resurrection of the Anointed One, Jesus. Daniel John Pouliot is alive and well. His story is not over; it's just beginning, to the praise, and honor, and glory of God!

CPSIA information can be obtained
at www.ICGtesting.com
Printed in the USA
BVHW030350041218
534656BV00003B/54/P